BEST OF IRISH

HOME BAKING

DELICIOUS MODERN RECIPES

Best of
Irish

BASED ON TRADITIONAL IRISH COOKING

Praise for the *Best of Irish* cookbooks:
'This series is fabulous and highly recommended. The books are
packed full of information ... A handy and very neat addition
to any kitchen shelf.'
Books Ireland
'Exciting Irish cookbook series.
Easy to follow, zippy and well presented'
Carla Blake, Irish Examiner
'An easy-to-carry-gift to bring home as a souvenir of a visit'
RTÉ Guide
'Sound recipes with an Irish flavour ...
And they are quite straightforward'
Georgina Campbell, Irish Independent

BIDDY WHITE LENNON is a founder member and former Chairwoman of the Irish Food Writers Guild. She is the author of several cookbooks, including four other titles in the *Best of Irish* series: *Meat Recipes*, *Traditional Cooking*, *Potato Recipes* and *Festive Cooking*. With Evan Doyle, she is also the author of *Wild Food – Nature's Harvest: How to Gather, Cook and Preserve*. She has written and presented a ten-part television series on healthy eating for the Irish Department of Health.

Biddy writes about food and cooking for the *Irish Farmers' Journal*, gives talks and cookery demonstrations all over Ireland and is consulted about food and cooking by producers and retailers. As a freelance journalist she contributes to many publications, including *Food & Wine Magazine*. She is a regular broadcaster on television and radio on subjects as varied as health, social welfare, fashion, interiors and travel.

As an actress, she is perhaps best known in Ireland for her portrayal of Maggie in the hugely popular RTÉ television series, *The Riordans*, a role she played for fifteen years. She continued to act in the series when it moved to radio and also co-wrote many episodes with her husband, later writing for the TV series *Glenroe*.

Best of
Irish

HOME
Baking

BIDDY WHITE LENNON

THE O'BRIEN PRESS
DUBLIN

First published 2003 by The O'Brien Press Ltd,
12 Terenure Road East, Rathgar, Dublin 6, Ireland.
Tel: +353 1 4923333; Fax: +353 1 4922777
E-mail: books@obrien.ie
Website: www.obrien.ie
Reprinted 2005, 2007, 2010, 2011 (twice, 2013), 2015.

ISBN: 978-0-86278-807-0

8 10 11 9
15 17 18 16

Editing, layout, typesetting, design: The O'Brien Press Ltd
Author photograph courtesy of Jenny McCarthy, Photosbyjen
Internal illustrations: Anne O'Hara
Photographs on back cover by Walter Pfeiffer
Printed and bound by CPI Group (UK) Ltd, Croydon, CR0 4YY
The paper in this book is produced using pulp from managed forests.

Contents

Desserts

Glossary

Introduction

No greater pleasure is available to people than the smell of home baking. It is the most deeply shared and deeply rooted communal sensation since we harnessed fire. Ground grains, flour mixed with water and other gathered ingredients, baked on a fire, near a fire, above it, below it, sheltered from it, within it (or any combination of these) is still the staple food of most regions of the world and continues to play a central, often ritual, role in many cultures and religions. The Irish are no different. However, the grains we found and which grow naturally in this green, wet land are different from those in other lands and our baking traditions are different because of this.

Wheat and barley have been cultivated in Ireland since Neolithic times. In the early Christian era the deliberately Spartan diet, with an emphasis on grains, fruits and vegetables rather than meat and dairy products, led to the widespread development of arable farming. Although soft wheat can be successfully grown in the wet Irish climate, oats were introduced during this period and, with barley, proved better suited to our climatic conditions. Oats became the principal grain crop and oaten bread the common bread of the people (barley, of course, has other, more 'spiritual' uses in Ireland and even then was used to make beer). Oat breads remained the principal breads eaten right up to the nineteenth century when unfortunates preparing for long voyages of emigration baked dry, flat oat-cakes to sustain them during the voyage.

Wheat bread was the bread of feast days and the tribute of chieftains and kings. In much later times, bread made from peas and beans (a common European tradition) was also seen amongst the poor and, during the great famines of the nineteenth century, a bread made from maize (referred to as 'yalla meal') was resorted to. However, although 'yalla meal' still sustains much of the world, it was not and is not relished by the Irish.

Baking techniques

In the larger monasteries and later in Norman castles and houses, bread was baked in ovens. But, until recent times, the ordinary people cooked and baked on the open hearth using a *lec* (a bake stone) or a *lan*, which was a flat griddle with two lugs (ears) set on a trivet, or hung over the embers. They also baked bread and tarts in a bastable, which was a large cast-iron pot with a flat lid. The cake of bread was set into the pot and the lid heaped with embers, – so providing heat from both top and bottom – similar to the American 'Dutch' oven. Dry, flat oat-cakes (intended for keeping) were baked on a wooden or metal stand (called a 'har'ning stand' in Ulster) set in front of the fire.

Ovens, when they arrived, were confined to small bakeries and the more prosperous houses. Usually they were a cavity in a wall, lined with bricks and sealed with a heavy cast-iron door. Using whatever fuel was to hand (turf, wood, furze bushes) a fire was lit and kept burning fiercely until the lining was very hot. Then the remains of the fire was brushed out and the bread put in to bake. Today, baking over an open fire or in the few remaining wall-ovens takes place mostly in the folk museums and parks dotted about the country to which tourists and schoolchildren go to marvel at our past. Meanwhile, modern Irish cooks bake in gas or electric cookers, or in state-of-the-art iron ranges fuelled by oil or gas.

In many parts of Ireland a loaf of bread is still called a 'cake'. This usage is a direct throwback to the old Scandinavian word for a flattish round of bread (of any grain, leavened or unleavened). The Vikings sailed on voyages of exploration and plunder and, in time, settled here and established towns around the Irish coast. They baked dry, flat oat breads called *kake* or *kaak* to sustain them on their journeys.

Leavening

In ancient times various forms of leavening (raising agent) were used. Barm was a by-product of beer brewing. Sowans, called 'bull's milk' in some parts of Ireland (but really the fermented juice of the husks of oats), was another traditional leavening for bread. A potato barm was got by grating potatoes and then allowing the juice to sour. These raising agents were sometimes used along with a sourdough but this was mainly in monasteries, 'big houses', inns, and bakeries in larger towns.

In the mid-eighteenth century Hannah Glass (in her book *The Art of Cookery made Plain and Easy*) credited the Dublin Society for obtaining for her the sourdough method of leavening bread in use in Ireland during the seventeenth and eighteenth centuries:

'Two pounds of dough from the last baking is kept in a wooden vessel covered well with flour. This is the leaven. The night before the next baking this was worked with a peck of flour and warm water and kept warm. By morning this dough will have risen and is enough to mix with two or three bushels of flour worked up with warm water and salt. The fresher the leaven the less sour the bread.' *Making bread without barm. Dublin Society, 1747.*

So, sourdough bread (but not too sour) seemed to be the taste of the time.

A different type of leavening in the bread mix was eventually supplied by the native Irish love of 'white meats' (dairy produce) and, in particular, of a variety of soured milk products. It is this amalgamation of soured milk or buttermilk and ground grains that makes Irish bread and baked goods stand out and win the hearts of visitors from the rest of continental Europe. What made it work was the use of soda, a combination that goes back a long way.

This quotation from a Butler manuscript receipt book of 1790 was printed in a book called *The Cookery and Cures of Old Kilkenny* which was published in 1983 to raise funds for the restoration St. Canice's Cathedral in that city. As the editors of the book remark, this is soda bread in one of its earliest forms – and the instructions are exemplary:

'Dissolve one teaspoon of super carbonate of soda in a wine glass full of spring water. Pour into a quart of buttermilk. To this add three quarts of flour. Mix all well together as quickly as possible, have your oven well heated and bake your loaf for one hour. The whole process before putting it in the oven, should occupy only three minutes.'

When commercial bicarbonate of soda (commonly called 'bread soda' in old recipes) became available it precipitated the abandonment of barm and sourdough as a leavening agent, particularly in domestic kitchens. It came into widespread use in the first half of the nineteenth century. Bicarbonate of soda is $NaHCO_3$, a salt formed when one of the two hydrogen atoms of carbonic acid is replaced by an atom of sodium. Its importance as an ingredient in Irish baking is that it interacts with the lactic acid of buttermilk and soured milk to release carbon dioxide into the dough. To this day a cake of soda bread remains 'the bread' of the

Irish people, whether baked in an Irish home, bought from a local bakery, from a country market, or in a supermarket (from a national bakery chain).

Bread is at the root of the Irish baking tradition, but the range of scones, tarts, cakes and biscuits baked in the home remains (especially in rural Ireland) simply astonishing. It is true that traditional Irish baking is on the plain side; the ability of a home baker to produce a good loaf of brown bread is far more highly-prized than fancy cakes. Not for us the confections developed in other European food cultures. Yet, when you consider the fairly limited range of ingredients used – wheat and oat flour, eggs, potatoes, honey, fresh fruits, berries and nuts that thrive in our climate, such as apples, pears, rhubarb, raspberries, strawberries, fraughans (similar to blueberries) and (given shelter) figs, hazelnuts and walnuts – and the subtle variations in flavour and texture, it remains a baking tradition to be proud of.

There are a number of reasons why home-baking has not died out. One reason is the baking competitions held at local agricultural shows – enthusiastic cooks enter up to a score of different categories and, while many protest that they 'just do it for the fun and to keep tradition alive', the competition is mighty! Another reason is the work of The Irish Countrywomen's Association whose members pass on traditional recipes and baking skills to each other and who take part in competitive baking contests. Another often unacknowledged influence has been the inspiration of renowned cookery writers like Florence Irwin in Northern Ireland and in the Republic Maura Laverty, Theodora Fitzgibbon, Paula Daly, Myrtle Allen, Georgina Campbell and Honor Moore.

A seamless handing on of this tradition came about with the founding of the Irish Food Writers Guild of which Theodora Fitzgibbon was the first president. As a founder member and current chairwoman, I freely declare my interest. Through the written word and by example, the guild encourages the tradition of home baking and works in harmony with Irish chefs (especially members of EuroToques whose aims include maintaining traditional dishes and methods of preparation) to support locally produced foods. Every year the guild celebrates the products of artisan food producers through The Irish Food Writers Guild Good Food Awards.

BROWN SODA BREAD

Called a 'cake' in many homes and just brown bread in others, this is the national loaf. It is made with varying amounts of wholemeal and plain white flour and (depending on the mood of the cook) small amounts of extra ingredients like wheat germ, wheat bran, oatmeal, or various seeds. Sometimes a small amount of butter, or even an egg, is added and occasionally, a little treacle /molasses. The exact amount of buttermilk needed depends on the flour and the weather – I mean it!

MAKES 1 loaf

Ingredients for the basic bread:

450 g/1 lb/3¾ US cups wholemeal wheat flour

175 g/6 oz/1½ cups plain white flour

1 teasp (generous) bicarbonate of soda

1 teasp salt

about 450 ml/15 fl oz/(scant) 2 US cups buttermilk

Method:

Pre-heat the oven to 200°C/400°F/Gas 6. The reaction of bicarbonate of soda and buttermilk is swift and the duration of their interaction short – speed is of the essence. Mix the flours, salt and soda in a mixing bowl. Add only enough buttermilk to make a soft dough. Flour your hands and the work surface and knead lightly (by hand, never with a machine) until the dough is smooth. It is important to understand that this is quite unlike making a yeast-risen dough. Shape into a circle about 4 cm/1½ inches deep. Take a sharp, well-floured knife and cut a deep cross in the top. Place on a baking sheet and bake for 40–45 minutes. To see if it is fully cooked test by tapping the bottom and listening for a hollow sound. Cool on a rack or, if you like a soft crust, wrapped in a linen or cotton tea-cloth. Eat the same day.

Variations:

A slightly more open texture may be achieved by adding two heaped tablespoons of wheat or oat bran and enough extra liquid to absorb the bran (about 60 ml/2 fl oz/¼ US cup).

Adding grains and seeds

There are probably as many 'secret' additions to the basic loaf of soda bread as there are home cooks (and chefs in restaurants who pride themselves on baking bread daily). Pinhead oatmeal and oatflakes are common additions, so too is wheat germ. While sesame seeds and sunflower seeds probably head the list of common additions today, caraway seeds have a long history in Irish baking, particularly in seed cake, sometimes known as Convent Cake probably because it continued to be made in Irish convents long after its popularity waned in ordinary households. Caraway seeds are still, occasionally, added to soda bread as a surprise extra.

WHITE SODA BREAD

In most parts of Ireland this bread is shaped and baked just like brown soda bread. However, in Ulster it is called a 'soda farl', and, rather than being shaped into a round loaf, it is usually rolled out into a flat round cake about 2 cm/¾ inch thick, then scored on both sides into four even sections called farls (quarters). The cake is then lightly dusted with flour and cooked slowly (turned once) on a griddle or a heavy frying pan until cooked through and light brown on both sides.

Ingredients:

625 g/1 lb 6 oz/5¼US cups plain white flour

1 teasp (generous) bicarbonate of soda

1 teasp salt

about 450 ml/15 fl oz/(scant) 2 US cups buttermilk

Method:

Pre-heat the oven to 200°C/400°F/Gas 6. Mix the flour, salt and soda in a mixing bowl. Add only enough buttermilk to make a soft dough. Flour your hands and the work surface and knead lightly by hand until the dough is smooth. Shape into a circle about 4 cm/1½ inches deep. Take a sharp, well-floured knife and cut a deep cross in the top. Place on a baking sheet and bake for 40–45 minutes. To see if it is fully cooked test by tapping the bottom and listening for a hollow sound. Cool on a rack or, if you like a soft crust, wrapped in a linen or cotton tea-cloth. Eat the same day.

Variations:

White fruit soda or curranty bread has about 110 g/4 oz/⅔ US cup (each) of sultanas and currants added.

Some cooks add a tablespoon of sugar (usually brown), or honey, or treacle. This last is by far the most traditional and gives a deeper, richer colour to the bread.

For Potato Bread, subtract one-third by weight of the flour and replace it with one-third (cooked weight) of freshly-cooked, mashed floury potato. A little extra buttermilk may be added to give a slightly wetter mixture.

ΜΑΚΙΝG A BUTTERMILK PLANT

While this is not real buttermilk, which is a by-product of butter-making, it makes a perfectly acceptable substitute if you live in a country where buttermilk is difficult to buy. It won't have the exactly the same flavour as the real thing but will behave in much the same way when used for baking. The principal is similar to making yoghurt at home. The plant will live indefinitely; there are tales, probably tall, of a plant living for almost a century. But because the plant must be fed every five days, it does tend to die off. Traditionally, you gave some to a friend or neighbour and if you neglected yours they would, in turn, give you some back.

Ingredients:

1 tablesp sugar

1 tablesp active dried yeast (not fast action)

600 ml/20 fl oz/ a generous 2½ US cups fresh milk

125 ml/4 fl oz/½ US cup boiling water

Method:

Mix the yeast with the sugar and a little warm water and leave in a warm place until it has reactivated and has a frothy top. Add boiling water to the milk and stir in the yeast mixture. Put the 'buttermilk' in a large screw top jar – at least 1½ litres/ 3 US pints. Place in a dark, warm place. Each day give the jar a gentle shake. After about 5 days it will be ready to use. Line a colander with butter muslin through which you have poured boiling water. Place this over a large bowl. Pour the mixture through the colander. The liquid that passes through is what is used for baking. Wash the curds that remain in the colander with warm water to remove any trace of the buttermilk. Return the curds to the (resterilised) jar. Mix the same quantity of fresh milk and boiling water used to start your original culture and add these to the jar with the curds. Cover with the lid and place in the same dark, warm place. The second batch tends to grow faster and may be ready for use again in a couple of days, although it will keep for longer. To keep your plant alive and sweet you must repeat the process at least every five days.

TREACLE BREAD

Treacle is a much loved flavouring especially in the Northern counties of the island. A by-product of sugar refining, it can range in colour from pale gold to almost black. In Ireland and Britain the paler varieties are called 'golden syrup', the darker ones 'treacle', which in other countries is more usually called 'molasses'.

MAKES 4 farls

Ingredients:

450 g/1 lb/4 US cups plain white unsifted flour

1 teasp salt

1 teasp bicarbonate of soda

2 tablesp treacle/molasses

300-375 ml/10-12 fl oz/1¼-1½ US cups buttermilk

Method:

Sift the flour, salt and bicarbonate of soda into a large bowl. Take a little of the buttermilk and the treacle and warm them together, stirring until the treacle is fully dissolved. Add this mixture and enough of the plain buttermilk to the flour to make a soft dough. The ability of flour to absorb liquid varies and on this depends the amount of buttermilk needed to achieve the correct consistency.

Knead lightly. Turn the dough out onto a floured work surface and shape into a round. With a sharp knife mark into four farls (triangles) and bake at 220°C/425°F/Gas 7 for 30–35 minutes or until the bread sounds hollow when lightly tapped on the base of the loaf.

'To know the colour of one's bread is to know one's place in society.'

An Irish saying.

Cheese Bread

*A quick and easy white soda bread that is akin to a scone mixture. It is a
forgiving mixture that can be made with either strong flour or plain white flour
and flavoured with whatever well-flavoured hard cheese you have in stock. It is
rather crumbly in texture and best eaten fresh, although it does make good toast.*

MAKES 1 loaf

Ingredients:

225 g/8 oz/2 US cups
(unsifted) white flour

1 teasp cream of tartar

½ teasp bicarbonate of soda

1 level teasp English mustard
powder

a pinch of salt

2 tablesp butter, cubed

150 ml/5 fl oz/²/₃ US cup
fresh milk

110 g/4 oz hard cheese, eg
Irish Gabriel Cheese or
extra mature Irish cheddar,
finely grated

2 teasp fresh sage, rosemary
or thyme, finely chopped
(optional)

Method:

Sift the flour, bicarbonate of soda, cream of
tartar, mustard powder and salt into a bowl.
Rub in the butter until you have a mixture
resembling breadcrumbs. Mix in
three-quarters of the grated cheese and the
herbs. Working quickly, stir in (lightly) just
enough milk to make a soft dough. Turn out
onto a floured work surface and knead very
lightly. Shape into a loaf about 20cm/8 inches
long or into a circle about 18cm/7 inches in
diameter. Place bread on a floured baking tray.
Brush the top with a little water and sprinkle
the remaining cheese evenly over the top.
Bake at 200°C/400°F/Gas 6 for about 20
minutes or until golden brown. The loaf
should be firm to the touch and sound hollow
when lightly tapped on the base. Cool on a
wire rack before cutting with a very sharp
knife.

Selection of Cheeses

whear yeast bread

Until the introduction of bicarbonate of soda, Irish bread was leavened either with barm, with sowans – a variety of home-produced yeasts – or using the sourdough system that prevailed in Europe. Made in large quantities in monasteries, castles, in the big houses, and in town bakeries, yeast breads were, as far as the common people were concerned, only for festive occasions. Today there are fewer small bakeries, but the tradition of yeast bread lives on with the surviving craft bakers and in those leading restaurants who pride themselves on baking their own breads. Alongside traditional brown soda bread you are likely to be offered a variety of yeast-risen breads and, following trends in continental Europe, these are likely to be flavoured with everything that grows under the sun: nuts, seeds, spices and the distinctly un-Irish sundried tomatoes. The basic yeast-risen loaf is much the same the world over: yeast, salt, water and strong flour (ground from hard wheat). The finest white loaf is made from unbleached white flour without the addition of any improvers or other additives. Fresh yeast is best, followed by active dried yeast. Quick or fast action yeasts are popular but do not produce the same quality of loaf as a slow-risen bread dough and, if combined with flour that contains improvers, you'll get a light airy loaf similar to commercial bread rather than the dense, well-flavoured, chewy bread produced by slow-rising.

Ingredients:

450 g/1 lb/4 US cups (un-sifted) strong unbleached flour

1 teasp salt

15 g/½ oz fresh yeast (or 7 g/¼ oz active dried yeast)

300 ml/10 fl oz/1¼ US cups warm water (roughly)

Method:

Activate the yeast in a little warm water (blood heat is the correct temperature) and leave in a warm (not hot) place until bubbles appear on the surface and create a light, frothy appearance. Place the flour in a warmed bowl and add the salt, the yeast mixture and most of the water. Stir the liquid into the flour and then begin to knead, lightly at first. If it feels dry add more liquid. The dough will be sticky to begin with, but as you knead it will gradually change texture. When it is silky to the touch and elastic in texture (in the old days this was described as the texture of a lady's silk stocking!) it is ready.

Kneading by hand will take about 10 minutes; far less if using the dough hook of an electric mixing machine. Fastest of all (but not best) is a food processor; if you are in a hurry, use one, but the dough will still need to be kneaded by hand for a few minutes.

Oil the dough lightly and set in a greased bowl, covered with cling film. Now leave in a warm (but not hot) place to rise. When it has doubled in size, give the dough a light punch with your fist (a process known as knocking down). Knead lightly again and shape for cooking. If you require a traditional loaf place it in a 900 g/2 lb loaf tin. Return to the warm place to prove. When the top rises to near the top of the tin it is ready to bake.

Bake at 200°C/400°F/Gas 6 for about 40 minutes or until the bottom sounds hollow when lightly tapped with the fingers. If you like a really crisp crust then you can turn the loaf out of the tin, place upside down on a rack in the oven and bake for a few more minutes. Cool on a wire rack and do not cut until completely cold.

Old Ways: In 1790 a Frenchman on a visit to Cork recorded: 'In the South of Ireland bread is made with oats, In Wicklow with rye and in Meath with a mix of rye and wheat.'

OATMEAL BREAD

Although now enjoying something of a comeback, the use of oatmeal in bread had all but died out when (many years ago) Honor Moore, a renowned food writer and a greatly treasured colleague, gave me this recipe. She pointed out something she had learned at her mother's knee in County Down, where traditional breads never went out of fashion, and later in the Belfast College of Domestic Science — that the oatmeal must be soaked overnight. The secret to this bread is soaking the oatmeal overnight in the buttermilk. A step you miss out at your peril!

MAKES 2 small loaves

Ingredients:

225 g/8 oz/1½ US cups fine oatmeal flour

225 g/8 oz/2 US cups strong white flour

725 ml/24 fl oz/3 US cups buttermilk

1 teasp bicarbonate of soda

1 teasp salt

2 teasp honey

Method:

Place the oatmeal flour in a large bowl. Warm the honey, add it to the buttermilk, mix lightly, then pour over the oatmeal flour. Leave to stand overnight in a cool place. The next morning, sift the white flour, salt and bicarbonate of soda over the soaked oatmeal flour. Quickly mix them together to get a fairly stiff dough. Knead lightly and very briefly. Because it is difficult to predict how much buttermilk the oatmeal flour will absorb, you may at this stage need to add a little more buttermilk. Divide the mixture into two well-greased, non-stick 450 g/1 lb loaf tins. Bake for 45–55 minutes at 200°C/400°F/Gas 6. The loaves are done when they sound hollow when lightly tapped on the base. If you like a hard, crisp crust cool them on a wire rack; if you prefer a soft crust, wrap them in a clean cloth while they cool.

NUT BREAD

In fine dining establishments, it has become a point of pride for our leading chefs to offer a selection of breads baked 'in house'. These will usually include a bread containing nuts — with the imported (and expensive) pistachio being commonest. This version uses either hazelnuts (a native tree) or walnuts (a tree which, although introduced, thrives in the Irish climate).

MAKES 2 small loaves

Ingredients:

15 g/½ oz active dried yeast

600 g/1 lb 5 oz/5¼ US cups strong white flour (or half white and half fine wholemeal)

1 teasp salt

30 g/1 oz/¼ stick butter

110 g/4 oz/1 US cup walnuts, or hazelnuts, roughly chopped

375 ml/12 fl oz/1½ US cups water, warmed to blood temperature

Method:

Dissolve the yeast in a little of the warm water and leave in a warm place until well-activated (frothy on top). Mix the flour and salt. Add the yeast liquid, the nuts, and almost all of the warm water (you may not need it all, so keep some back). Mix well and knead until the dough is elastic, smooth, and silky to the touch, adding a little more water, or flour, as you need it. Place in a bowl oiled with a little walnut oil and cover with cling film. Leave to rise in a warm place for 1–1½ hours (or until at least doubled in size). Knock down. Knead again for a few minutes. Divide into two pieces and shape into two rolls. Place on an oiled baking tray. Cover with a dampened cloth. Leave to prove in a warm place for about an hour, or until doubled in size. Uncover. Using a razor-sharp knife make slashes across the tops. Bake at 220°C/425°F/Gas 7 for about 10 minutes. Lower the heat to 190°C/375°F/Gas 5 and continue baking for another 25–30 minutes. The bread is done when golden brown and it sounds hollow when lightly tapped on the base of the loaf. Cool on a wire rack.

CARROT AND DILLISK BREAD

Gerry Galvin, poet, dreamer and one of Ireland's leading and most innovative chefs, created this lovely savoury bread (illustrated on inside front cover). A traditional Irish seaweed savour, dillisk (also known as dulse) lends a taste of the sea and the carrot a hint of sweetness that makes it acceptable as a teabread.

MAKES 1 loaf

Ingredients:

30 g/1 oz dried dillisk, soaked for 5 minutes in water

110 g/4 oz/1 stick butter, melted

1 large carrot, grated

4 medium eggs

60 g/2 oz/scant ¼ US cup caster sugar

a pinch of salt

255 g/9 oz/2 generous US cups plain white, unsifted flour

1 ½ teasp baking powder

Method:

Drain the dillisk and pat dry with kitchen paper; chop finely. Brush the inside of a 900 g/2 lb loaf tin using a little of the melted butter. In a bowl, combine the remaining butter, grated carrot, eggs, sugar, dillisk and salt. Sift the flour and baking powder together and fold into the mixture. Place in the loaf tin, smooth the top and bake at 200°C/400°F/Gas 6 for 50 minutes, or until a skewer inserted into the centre of the loaf comes out clean. Cool in the tin before turning out. Best eaten fresh.

POTATO BREAD ROLLS

Two cultures collide in this unusual recipe by renowned food writer and food historian, the late Theodora Fitzgibbon: the yeast bread of the large houses and town bakers and the potato of the common people. The rolls are light, moist and freeze well.

MAKES 15 rolls

Ingredients:

110 g/4 oz floury potatoes, warm

15 g/½ oz active dried yeast

60 g/2 oz/scant ¼ US cup sugar

450 g/1 lb/4 US cups unsifted plain white flour, warmed

1 teasp salt

60 g/2 oz/½ stick butter, cut into small pieces

150 ml/5 fl oz/²/₃ US cup milk, warmed

150 ml/5 fl oz/²/₃ US cup water, warmed

1 medium egg, beaten

extra milk for glazing

Method:

Cook the potatoes in salted water. Drain, reserving 2 tablesp of the cooking liquid. Peel and while still hot process the potatoes with a potato ricer or food mill. Keep warm. Add the yeast and one teaspoon of sugar to the lukewarm potato liquid and leave in a warm place until frothy. Meanwhile sift the flour and salt into a bowl. Rub in the butter. Make a well in the centre, then add the rest of the sugar and the warm potato and mix well. Combine the yeast mixture with the warm milk and the egg and about half the warm water (you may not need all of it). Knead very well until you have a smooth, softish dough, adding more water if necessary. Cover and leave in a warm place to rise. It will take about an hour to double in size. Knock down on a well-floured surface; knead and shape into rolls. Place on greased baking trays, leaving plenty of space beween each roll. Cover with a cloth and allow to prove for 20 minutes. Brush lightly with a little milk. Bake at 220°C/425°F/Gas 7 for 15–20 minutes until golden brown and sounding hollow when tapped lightly on the base. The rolls are best eaten fresh; however, they also freeze well.

WATERFORD BLAAS

These light, soft-crusted, floury, morning rolls are eaten warm for breakfast in County Waterford and nowhere else in Ireland. Tradition in Waterford has it that the name derives from a word used by Huguenots (who fled religious persecution in France and settled in Waterford) when asking for white flour, for which the French word is blé. The way a native of Waterford pronounces the word 'blaa' – bleh – is very similar to the French pronunciation. Blaas are widely available from Waterford bakeries and are now only home-baked by emigrés who long for the taste of home. This recipe is the closest you'll get to the traditional blaa for a domestic oven.

MAKES 24

Ingredients:

1.4 kg/3 lbs strong white flour

60 g/2 oz fresh yeast (or 30 g/ 1 oz active dried yeast)

1 teasp sugar

300 ml/10 fl oz/1¼ US cups warm water

600 ml/1 imperial pint/2¼ US pints water

2 teasp salt

Method:

Dissolve the yeast and sugar in the warm water. When the yeast is frothy and the sugar dissolved add to the flour with salt and remaining water. Knead for 5 minutes until smooth and elastic. Put into a large oiled bowl and cover with oiled cling film. Let it prove in a warm place until doubled in size (about 1 hour). Knock it down and let it prove again in the same way for half an hour. Knock down gently. Divide into 24 even-sized, round, slightly flattened buns (use a scales if you haven't got a perfect eye) each weighing 90g/3 oz. Put these on a floured baking tray and let them rise slowly at room temperature until doubled in size (2 to 3 hours). Dust with a light sifting of flour. Set the oven to 220°C/425°F/Gas 7. Bake for about 15 minutes or until they sound hollow when tapped gently. The rolls should not be too brown on top.

Waterford's favourite way of eating blaas today is to fill a large-sized commercial blaa with a full fry, making a portable and substantial breakfast.

BOXTY ON THE GRIDDLE

'Boxty on the griddle,
Boxty in the pan
If you don't eat your boxty
You'll never get a man.'

And the answering rhyme chanted by the young women is instructive:

'I'll have none of your boxty
I'll have none of your blarney
But I'll whirl my petticoats over my head
And be off with my royal Charlie.'

Boxty is perhaps the most individual of our traditional potato dishes. It differs
from other European dishes using grated raw potato in that cooked mashed potato
and flour are also added. It is particularly associated with the northern midlands
and the province of Ulster. Boxty must be cooked as soon as it is prepared lest the
raw potatoes turn black.

MAKES 2 large rounds, 4 farls, or 8 small squares

Ingredients:

450 g/1 lb raw floury
potatoes, peeled and grated

450 g/1 lb cooked floury
potatoes, mashed while
warm

110 g/4 oz/1 US cup unsifted
plain white flour

2 teasp salt

Method:

Grate the raw potatoes directly into a clean cloth. Holding the cloth over a bowl, twist the ends of the cloth together tightly and wring out all the starchy liquid from the potatoes into the bowl. The wrung potatoes are placed in another bowl and covered with the mashed potatoes (this prevents the grated potatoes becoming discoloured). The liquid in the first bowl settles and the starch drops to the bottom. Carefully pour off the clear liquid at the top. Then mix the starch thoroughly with the grated and mashed potatoes. Finally flour is sifted with the salt, mixed in, and kneaded as if you were kneading bread dough. This is rolled out on to a floured board until about 1.5 cm/½ inch thick. Cut into farls (triangles), squares, or circles.

Heat a heavy griddle (or frying pan) which has been very lightly greased. Cook the boxty cakes slowly until well browned on both sides. They are best eaten hot, fresh from the pan, lightly buttered.

Traditionally boxty cakes were fried in bacon fat for breakfast. If this is your plan you might make them thicker and then slice each cake in two horizontally before frying.

the Full Irish, with Boxty

BOXTY IN THE PAN

A good deal more flour is used in this recipe, and also buttermilk together with bicarbonate of soda. The resulting mixture makes boxty potato pancakes.

MAKES about 20

Ingredients:

255 g/9 oz floury potatoes, grated raw

255 g/9 oz floury potatoes, cooked , then peeled and mashed while warm

255 g/9 oz/2¼ US cups plain white flour or finely ground wholewheat flour

½ teasp bicarbonate of soda

300-400 ml/10-14 fl oz/(generous)1¼-1½ US cups of buttermilk

Method:

Extract the starch in exactly the same way as for griddle boxty and mix it with the grated raw potatoes and the cooked mashed potatoes. Sift the flour, salt and bicarbonate of soda and mix thoroughly into the potatoes. Add enough buttermilk to make a thick pancake batter. Season with salt and freshly ground black pepper. Cook at once. Drop spoonfuls – just enough to form small cakes about 8 cm/3 inches across – onto a heated, lightly-greased pan and cook until cooked through and well browned on each side.

Eat hot from the pan with butter and honey.

OVEN-BAKED BOXTY

The addition of fat and baking powder produces something nearer to a scone.

MAKES about 15–20 small scones

Ingredients:

255 g/9 oz floury potatoes, grated raw

255 g/9 oz floury potatoes, cooked and mashed

255 g/9 oz/2¼ cups plain white flour

½ teasp baking powder

2 tablesp melted bacon fat, or butter

a little buttermilk, or fresh milk

salt

Method:

Sift the flour, baking powder, and a good pinch of salt together and make exactly as you would griddle boxty but adding the bacon fat or butter. Add just enough milk or buttermilk to make a firm dough. Divide in two pieces, roll out on a floured board, then divide into farls or cut into circles with a scone cutter. Arrange on a greased baking tray. Bake at 180°C/350°F/Gas 4 for 30–40 minutes. Eat hot from the oven, split and buttered.

Spin-dried boxty:

I must thank fellow food writer and historian Marion Maxwell of Enniskillen for this tall, but entirely true, tale. She wrote in *The Impartial Observer* about a friend, Jackie Owens of Bellanaleck, who found the task of wringing out the grated raw potatoes in a cloth too much trouble and devised an easier method. Jackie puts the grated potato in a pillowcase, knots the top, then whizzes it in an electric spin-dryer and saves herself a good deal of elbow grease. It's certainly inventive and easier on the arms, but you do have to sacrifice the starch that collects at the bottom of the potato water, which some people (myself included) think can't properly be left out.

potato cakes

A potato cake is a savoury cake, not a sweet one. The texture varies from region to region, depending on the quantity of flour used. Commercial potato cakes are of the firm, well-floured variety – to make them easy to handle and ensure a longer shelf-life. More potato and less flour makes a moister cake which is more tender to the tooth. Thickness varies from ¼-½ inch; cakes high in potato are thicker than those high in flour. Just to complicate this arcane craft even more, you should know that in the northeast of Ireland these cakes are usually called 'fadge' or 'tatie squares' (even when cut into triangular farls!). Whatever about the relative merits of the shape, it's a recipe worth experimenting with to find one most to your taste. One way or the other, potato cakes are an essential part of an 'Ulster Fry' but not, strangely enough, of 'the Full Irish' breakfast.

MAKES 2–6 depending on size and thickness

Ingredients:

450 g/1 lb floury potatoes, cooked, and mashed hot

60-175 g/2-6 oz/½-1½ US cups plain white flour

½ teasp salt

2 tablesp butter, melted

60 ml/2 fl oz/¼ US cup milk (approx.)

Method:

Keep back a couple of tablespoons of the flour. Mix all the ingredients together, adding just enough milk to make a fairly firm dough. Sprinkle the reserved flour on a flat surface and roll the dough out until it is ¼–½ inch thick. Cut into a shape and size that pleases you. Bake on an ungreased griddle (or heavy frying pan) until lightly brown on both sides. Serve hot from the pan, or reheat by frying in just a little bacon fat or butter; or grill until warmed through, spread with a very small amount of butter.

POTATO AND OAT CAKES

These substantial potato cakes have different names in different parts of Ireland: potato and oat cakes in the South, oaten potato cakes in Ulster (except in County Antrim where, according to the food writer Florence Irwin, 'the Cookin' Woman', they are always called Rozel. She notes wryly that they are 'not suitable for invalids'.

MAKES 2–4 depending on size and thickness

Ingredients:

350 g/12 oz floury potatoes, cooked and mashed hot

110 g/4 oz/1 generous US cup pinhead oatmeal

2 tablesp butter

a good pinch of salt

Method:

Mix everything together, using a drop of milk if it seems necessary. Roll out, shape and cook in the same manner as potato cakes (p. 28).

'Rye bread will do you good
Barley bread will do you no harm
Wheaten bread will sweeten your blood
Oaten bread will strength your arm'

BARM BRACK

Brack, our traditional fruit bread, has been a festive dish since ancient times. It was eaten at Lughnasa, the first day of autumn and the start of the harvest, at Samhain, the first day of winter, at Imbolc (St Brigid's Day) the first day of spring and at Beltane, the first day of summer. All Souls' Night (Hallowe'en) may now have supplanted the pre-Christian festival of Samhain, but it's still the night on which brack is always eaten in Ireland. A ring is placed in the brack to herald marriage the following spring for whoever finds it. In Cork (always wanting to go one better) they also put in a dried pea for spinsterhood, a bean for riches, a rag for poverty, and a piece of matchstick, which predicts that your husband will beat you! There are two versions of the origin of the name barm brack: that it comes from the Irish bairgain breac – bread that is speckled; or that it derives from the use of barm, or yeast drawn off fermenting malt. Brack made at home, as often as not, is raised not with yeast but with baking powder and is called a tea brack because the dried fruit is soaked in tea. A barm brack, on the other hand, is raised with yeast (but not barm) and is bought from a bakery rather than baked at home. Both types are eaten sliced and buttered.

Ingredients:

255 g/9 oz/1 ¼ US cups raisins

255 g/9 oz/1 ½ US cups sultanas

60 g/2 oz/scant ¼ US cup mixed peel (optional)

225 g/8 oz/1 generous US cup dark cane sugar

500 ml/16 fl oz/2 US cups Indian tea, hot, strong and black

350 g/12 oz/3 US cups (unsifted) plain white flour

2 teasp baking powder

1 teasp mixed spice

2 medium-sized eggs, beaten

a little honey for the glaze

a 20 cm/8 inch cake tin (at least 7.5 cm/3 inches deep) greased and lined with greaseproof (unwaxed) or non-stick paper

Method:

Place the fruit, sugar and peel in a bowl and pour the hot tea (without milk) over them; stir well until the sugar is dissolved, then stand overnight. Sift flour, baking powder and spice. Mix, alternately, some egg and some fruit into the flour, stirring thoroughly. When all the egg and fruit has been mixed in, add the ring and other charms if you are using them, making sure they are evenly distributed throughout the mix. For safety, wrap them in greaseproof paper.

Turn out the mixture into the prepared cake tin and bake at 160°C/325°F/Gas 3 for about 1½ hours. About 10 minutes before it is ready, brush the top of the brack with warmed honey. Return to the oven until fully cooked. Cool in the tin for 15 minutes before turning out (glazed side up) on to a rack to cool. It keeps well in a tin for 4–5 days.

Cook's Tip:

Leftover brack may be used for the rich Brack and Butter Pudding on p. 68. It is also very good toasted and buttered.

Barm brack

CRUMPETS

Crumpets are a gorgeous afternoon tea snack on a cold winter's day.

MAKES about 10

Ingredients:
For the first mixing:

225 g/8 oz/2 US cups strong white flour

225 g/8 oz/2 US cups plain white flour

7 g/¼ oz active dried yeast

600 ml/20 fl oz/2¼ US cups milk and water mixed

1 tablesp salt

1 teasp sugar

2 tablesp vegetable oil

For the second mixing:

½ teasp bicarbonate of soda

150 ml/5 fl oz/⅔ US cup warm water

extra oil or butter for greasing the crumpet rings

Method:

Warm the flour in an ovenproof bowl for about five minutes in the oven (at 110°C/225°F/Gas ¼). Warm the oil, milk, water and sugar just to blood temperature and use a little of it to activate the dried yeast. Leave the yeast in a warm place for about 10 minutes. Mix the flour and salt, then, quickly, add the yeast mixture followed by the rest of the liquids. Mix the batter with great vigour until it is smooth and elastic. Cover the bowl and leave it to rise in a warm place until the surface is covered with bubbles (typically, this will take 1½–1¾ hours). Knock down the batter with a wooden spoon. Dissolve the bicarbonate of soda in the second amount of warm water and stir this into the batter at once. Cover the bowl again and allow to rise in a slightly warmer place. To cook the crumpets, take a griddle, or a large, heavy, well-seasoned frying pan. Grease whatever number of crumpet rings (about 9 cm/3½ inches in diameter and 2.5 cm/1 inch deep) you can easily fit into this. Place the rings in the pan or on the griddle and heat over a very low heat for about 5 minutes. Pour enough batter into each ring to come almost to the top. Cook gently over the same low heat until the top of the crumpet forms a skin. This will take 7–10 minutes and there should be a lot of tiny holes on the surface (if not, your batter may be a little too thick, so add a little warm water before cooking the next batch). The underside should be set smooth and be golden in colour. Slip off the rings and flip the crumpet over and cook for 3 minutes on the second side. Keep this batch warm (in a folded cloth in a warm place, or in a covered dish in the oven) while you cook the rest.

Crumpets should be eaten fresh with butter and jam; but some people like their crumpets split and toasted – traditionalists think this makes them tough and changes the experience in the mouth.

Old Ways: 'She scalded the meal with salted boiling water, made it into a dough, rolled it thinly, and cut it into little scones. A bed was made on the hearth, by racking the ashes. Each scone was wrapped in a cabbage leaf, placed on the bed with hot ashes piled on top and left until cooked. The scorched leaf was turned back to disclose fragrant little cakes which were delicious with rasher gravy and an egg yolk.'

Ash Cakes (described by Maura Laverty who claimed her grandmother made them in 1920)

MUFFINS

This is a traditional tea cake and no relation to the American muffin. In America this small cake is known as an 'English muffin'. There is a wealth of lore attached to muffins: they go hard and stale as they cool; ideally they should be eaten as soon as they are cooked, pulled gently apart (never cut with a knife; this makes them tough); they are buttered while hot so that the butter melts; if they have been allowed to cool they are toasted on both sides, opened out and then buttered. Even then they should be kept warm, a requirement that caused muffin fanciers to invent a special covered dish to keep them warm at the afternoon tea table.

MAKES 8

Ingredients:

450 g/1 lb/4 US cups strong flour (or half strong and half plain white flour)

7 g/¼ oz/1 teasp active dried yeast

1 level tablesp salt

½ teasp sugar

2 tablesp olive oil, or clarified butter, or lard

450 ml/15fl oz/2 scant US cups equal quantities milk and water

2–3 tablesp rice flour

Method:

First warm the flour in an oven at 140°C/275°F/Gas 1 for 8–10 minutes. Do not on any account skip this step; it is the warmed flour together with the fat that gives the dough the characteristic texture that makes a muffin a muffin. Mix the milk, water and fat and warm to blood temperature. Use a little of this liquid, together with the sugar, to reactivate the dried yeast. When this is frothy, mix the flour, salt and liquid together (it's a wet dough so this is best done with a wooden spoon or the dough hook of a heavy-duty electric mixer). When elastic and smooth, cover and leave to rise at 21°C/70°F for about 50 minutes.

Divide dough into 8 pieces and, using rice flour for dusting, shape each into a round. Place on a non-stick baking tray well dusted with rice flour. Shape the sides of each piece so that they are evenly square in shape (rather than round). Cover with a cloth or a large piece of cling film and leave to prove at room temperature for about 40 minutes.

Heat a griddle (or a large, heavy frying pan) over a gentle heat. Using a palette knife (or a fish slice) transfer as many muffins as will fit while leaving space between each to allow them to be turned easily. Cook slowly over a low heat. They will take about 8–10 minutes on each side. They should be light golden-brown on each side with a band of white in the middle. The height will be 4-5 cm/1½-2 inches. The exterior should be lightly crusty and the interior when split open will have the open texture of a honycomb. If they are to be eaten at once keep them warm in a folded cloth, or in a low oven. As they cool, muffins go hard and stale and must be toasted before tearing apart and buttering.

Griddle Pan

Hot Cross Buns

Traditionally eaten on Good Friday, the Friday before Easter Sunday. The cross on the top is the Christian symbol, a reminder that this was the day Jesus was crucified.

MAKES 12

Ingredients:
For the dough:

450 g/1 lb/4 cups unsifted strong white flour

7 g/¼ oz/1 teasp quick-action yeast

a good pinch of salt

½ teasp ground cinnamon

1 teasp mixed spice/allspice

½ teasp nutmeg, grated

90 g/3 oz/½ US cup sultanas

90 g/3 oz/(scant) ½ US cup currants

30 g/1 oz/1 tablesp mixed peel, chopped (optional)

1 medium-sized egg, beaten

250 ml/8 fl oz/1 US cup full-fat milk

For the crosses:

2 tablesp butter

45 g/1½ oz/⅓ US cup flour

a little cold water

Method:

Mix the flour, yeast, salt, spices and dried fruit together. Add the egg and enough milk to make a soft dough (you may need more or less liquid). Knead the dough until really smooth to the touch and elastic in texture; by hand this will take 10 minutes, using dough hooks and an electric mixer rather less time (and considerably less effort). Divide into 12 pieces and shape into round buns. Place on a well-greased baking tray leaving enough room for each bun to expand. Cover and prove at (warm) room temperature until they have risen and reached twice their original size.

Make the dough for the crosses by rubbing softened butter into flour and wetting with just enough water to make a soft dough. Roll out thinly and cut into narrow strips. Wet the underside of each strip and place two strips on each bun in the shape of a cross. Bake at 200°C/400°F/Gas 6 for 25–30 minutes They should be well-risen and browned and, when the bottom of a bun is tapped lightly, it should sound hollow. Serve freshly cooked, with butter.

BUTTERMILK SCONES

Scones are the great standby of the Irish country kitchen. They can be made in a few minutes and eaten warm from the oven. With imagination, a plain scone can be transformed into a variety of sweet and savoury breads.

MAKES 8–12

Ingredients:

450 g/1 lb/4 US cups plain white flour

1 (scant) teasp bicarbonate of soda (bread soda)

1 (scant) teasp baking powder

1 teasp salt

90 g/3 oz/³/₄ stick butter, cubed

1 egg, beaten (optional)

about 200ml/7 fl oz/1 scant US cup buttermilk

Method:

Sift the flour, salt, bicarbonate of soda and baking powder together. Rub in the butter until the texture resembles breadcrumbs. Quickly and lightly mix in the egg and milk, using enough liquid to make a soft dough that is puffy and easy to roll out. Knead lightly – no more than six times. Roll out to 2–2½ cm/¾–1 inch thick (depending on how high and moist you prefer the finished scone). For even rising, cut out the scones with a fluted cutter dipped in flour, or with a very sharp knife. Transfer to a baking sheet with a palette knife. Bake immediately at 220°C/425°F/Gas 7 for 15–20 minutes, or until well risen and brown.

Variations:

Savoury: Use half plain white and half fine-ground wholemeal flour.
Add 175 g/6 oz/1¼ US cups grated hard cheese (extra mature Cheddar, Gabriel from the West Cork Cheese Company), or Parmesan.
Brush with milk and sprinkle about 2 tablesp of poppy seeds over the top.

Sweet: Mix in 1 tablespoon of sugar and 3 or 4 tablespoons of sultanas.
Mix in 1–2 finely chopped dessert apples (peeled and cored) and a teaspoon of ground nutmeg (or cinnamon).
Add about six moist dried apricots, finely chopped.

BUTTERMILK AND OAT DROP SCONES

Fine-ground oatmeal may be hard to find; a health food shop is the most likely source. However, it's easy enough to grind pinhead oatmeal in a food processor or a coffee grinder.

MAKES about 20

Ingredients:

600 ml/20 fl oz/2⅜ US cups buttermilk

175 g/6 oz/1¼ US cups fine-ground oatmeal

90 g/3 oz/¾ US cup unsifted white self-raising flour

2 tablesp honey

1 teasp bicarbonate of soda

1 medium egg, beaten

a little extra milk to thin the batter

Method:

Put the oatmeal in a bowl. Add the buttermilk, mix well, then leave to soak overnight. Just before cooking, sift together the flour and bicarbonate of soda and add these to the oatmeal mixture. Add the egg, honey and enough milk to make a thinnish batter (just a little thinner than you would use for ordinary pancakes).

Heat a heavy, well-seasoned griddle or pan over a medium heat. When it is hot, drop in tablespoonfuls of the batter, well spaced. Cook until they rise, are covered in bubbles on the upper side and are golden brown underneath. Turn and brown the other side. By far the best way to eat these is hot from the pan with a little butter and honey. However, golden syrup with a little whipped cream is pretty good.

yalla meal scones

In Ireland 'yalla meal' is forever associated with the potato famines. Imported as a substitute for potatoes and flour, cornmeal was not highly regarded, and, once the necessity to use it receded, was rarely used except in Northern Ireland where it remained in use a hundred years later as 'Indian meal'. This classic recipe is by Florence Irwin, a travelling instructor in domestic economy a century ago in County Down, where she was known as 'the cookin' woman' by the countrywomen she taught. They, in turn, gave her their recipes. Florence Irwin faithfully recorded these and published them for over fifty years in her newspaper column in The Northern Whig and in two famous books: Irish Country Recipes and The Cookin' Woman.

MAKES 14–16

Ingredients:

225 g/8 oz/1 ¼ US cups cornmeal/maize flour

225 g/8 oz/2 US cups plain white flour

½ teasp bicarbonate of soda

½ teasp cream of tartar

½ teasp salt

1 tablesp caster sugar

60 g/2 oz lard

About 250 ml/8 fl oz/1 US cup buttermilk

Method:

Place the cornmeal/maize flour in a bowl. Sift in the white flour, salt, bicarbonate of soda, cream of tartar and sugar together and mix well. Rub in the lard and add just enough buttermilk to make a soft dough. Knead quickly and lightly. Roll out until about 2.5 cm/1 inch thick. Cut into 5 cm/2 inch squares and bake at once at 220°C/425°F/Gas 7 for about 13–16 minutes or until the scones are golden brown and sound hollow when you tap the base lightly. You may also cook these in the traditional way on a griddle or in a heavy pan over a medium heat.

Split gently with the tip of a pointed knife and serve hot with butter.

apple fadge

In County Antrim the many small bakeries that were once famous all over Ulster used to make this. The origins of the word are unknown — it is neither Gaelic nor, apparently, Ulster-Scots. It is used variously to denote a thick wheaten loaf, a potato cake baked on the griddle, or a large piece of oatcake. Here, and in the small bakeries where it was once made, it means a savoury potato cake stuffed with apples.

MAKES 4

Ingredients:

450 g/1 lb/3 US cups floury potatoes cooked, mashed and still hot

a good pinch of salt

2 tablesp butter

110 g/4 oz/1 US cup unsifted plain, white flour

8 fl oz/1 US cup cooked fluffy apple purée

Method:

Mix the potatoes, flour, butter, and salt together and knead lightly. Divide into 4 and roll out into 4 circles. Divide the apple purée evenly between them, placing it on one side of the circle only. Fold the other side over, as if you were making a turnover, or pasty. Seal the edges well by pinching together firmly, so they do not open while cooking. Place on a baking try and bake at 200°C/400°F/Gas 6 for about 20 minutes, or until brown and crisp. Serve hot.

These cakes are good with grilled sausages, or with pork, duck, or goose.

Cook's Tip:

Although Bramley apples provide the fluffiest purée, it is quite a sour apple which you may like to season with a little sugar.

POTATO PASTRY

An excellent shortcrust pastry can be made by substituting cooked potatoes for some of the flour. Like all pastries the recipes vary. The first is very rich and fat-heavy, but produces a light crust suitable for fruit or savoury pies or as a base for small tarts; the second uses just half the butter but is enriched with an egg – less delicate, but easier to handle and roll out.

MAKES enough pastry for 1 pastry case or pastry crust

Ingredients:

110 g/4 oz/1 US cup unsifted self-raising flour

110 g/4 oz/²/₃ US cup (cooked weight) floury, peeled, cooked potatoes, still hot

175 g/6 oz/1½ sticks butter, very cold

pinch salt

water (only if needed)

Variation:

110 g/4 oz/¾ US cup floury potatoes cooked and hot

110 g/4 oz/1 US cup unsifted plain white flour

½ teasp baking powder

pinch salt

90 g/3 oz/¾ stick butter

Method 1:

Put the hot potatoes through a potato ricer or mouli and allow to cool. Sift the flour and salt. Rub the butter into the flour and then, as lightly as possible, mix in the potato. Add water, if necessary, to get a firm dough. Knead lightly and roll out as you would for shortcrust pastry.

Method 2:

Put the hot potatoes through a potato ricer or mouli and allow to cool. Sift flour, salt and baking powder together. Rub in the butter, stir in the potatoes lightly and just enough beaten egg to make a firm dough. Roll out on a floured board and use for both sweet and savoury dishes.

RHUBARB TART

A classic Irish tart filling during spring and early summer. The rhubarb patch survives in gardens all over the country and rhubarb remains a favourite filling for tarts as well as being used for jams and preserves. Fruit tarts in Ireland generally have both a top and bottom crust (rather like an American pie).

SERVES 4–6

Ingredients:

900 g/2 lb rhubarb

110 g/4 oz/1 generous US cup sugar

1 egg white, beaten until stiff

Potato pastry for a crust for both top and bottom (Use double the quantity of the second variation of potato pastry on page 41)

Method:

Clean and cut up the rhubarb into short lengths. Place in a pan with the sugar and simmer for about 10 minutes or until the rhubarb is barely tender. Fold in the egg white and cool.

Line a 20–25 cm/8–10 inch flan or tart tin with half the pastry. Spoon (or pour) the filling into the pastry case and top with the remaining pastry. Bake at 200°C/400°F/Gas 6 for 40–50 minutes until the pastry is cooked through and golden brown.

Serve warm with whipped cream.

Pie (potato pastry)

apple tart

Apple tart is probably the most popular Irish family favourite, eaten as a dessert, for afternoon tea, or as a late night snack, and served with cream, ice cream, custard, or even with a hunk of cheese. Cloves are the traditional flavouring, but leave them out if you don't like their distinctive taste. If you like the taste but not the texture use a pinch of ground cloves. The Irish like a filling with a fluffy texture, achieved by using a variety of cooking apple called Bramley. If you prefer the apple slices to remain intact, use the variety called Granny Smith. You may find the pastry used here too rich; a plain shortcrust pastry may be substituted.

Ingredients:

For a rich sweet pastry:

225 g/8 oz/2 US cups unsifted plain white flour

110 g/4 oz/1 stick butter, cubed

60 g/2 oz/(scant) ¼ US cup caster sugar

1 medium egg

1-2 teasp cold water

for the filling:

700 g/1½ lb cooking apples

150 g/5 oz/¾ US cup caster sugar

6 whole cloves

Method:

Sift flour into a bowl. Rub in the butter with your fingertips as quickly and lightly as possible. Stir in the sugar and mix it in well. Add the egg and mix in using a flat-bladed knife, adding a little water if it seems necessary to make a firm dough. Wrap and chill for about 20 minutes before rolling out. When ready to bake, peel, core and slice the apples. Leaving about a third of the pastry to one side, roll out the rest quite thinly and use it to line a greased tart tin about 20cm/8 inches in diameter. Arrange the apples evenly on the pastry; add the cloves and sugar. Roll out the remaining pastry and carefully set it on top of the filling. Seal the edges well. Brush the top lightly with a little milk and sprinkle with a little caster sugar. Bake at 190°C/375°F/Gas 5 for 35–40 minutes, or until the top is golden brown and crisp. If it browns too quickly you can cover it loosely with a piece of tinfoil or reduce the heat slightly. Serve hot or cold with whipped cream or custard.

ßakeð cheesecake

Soft curd cheeses were but one of scores of bán bhianna (white meats) that were once staples of the Irish diet. Then, for historical reasons, they all but died out. The revival of farmhouse cheesemaking over 30 years ago has led to the development of upwards of three score different varieties of Irish farm cheeses, many with an international reputation. Curd cheese is a fresh, smooth, creamy, soft cheese which once was eaten only in summer. Today it is made from cow, goat, or sheep milk and there are many enticing varieties to choose from, including Kockalara fresh sheep's milk cheese and Old MacDonnell's Farm fresh goat's milk cheese.

SERVES 6–8

Ingredients:
For the shortcrust pastry:

175 g/6 oz/1½ US cups unsifted plain white flour

110 g/4 oz/1 stick butter, cut into small cubes

cold water to mix

For the filling:

225 g/8 oz soft fresh cheese

2 medium eggs, beaten

90 g/3 oz/scant ½ US cup caster sugar

juice and finely grated zest of 1 lemon

2 teasp cornflour

1 tablesp butter, melted

60 g/2 oz/scant ½ US cup raisins (soaked for 10 minutes in hot water, then drained)

For the topping:

1 tablesp icing sugar

Method:

Rub the butter into the flour until the mixture is like breadcrumbs. Add the water a tablespoonful at a time using only enough to give a firm dough. Turn out unto a floured work surface and knead lightly until smooth and silky. Cover with cling film and chill for 20–30 minutes. Roll the pastry out thinly to fit a 23 cm/9 inch loose-bottomed, fluted-edged flan or tart tin.

To bake blind, prick the bottom of the pastry case with a fork. Line the pastry case with a piece of greaseproof paper, cut 5 cm/2 inches larger than the tin and press it against the edges of the pastry. Fill with dried beans or rice and bake for 15 minutes at 190°C/375°F/Gas 5 (or until the base is firm). Remove the paper and beans, then return to the oven to bake for 5 more minutes.

Blend the cornflour with 2 tablespoons of the lemon juice and set aside. Beat together the curd cheese, caster sugar, eggs, lemon zest and remaining juice. Beat the cornflour and lemon juice, together with the melted butter, into the cheese mixture. Tip the mixture into the pastry case and sprinkle with the raisins. Bake at 190°C/375°F/Gas 5 for 30–35 minutes until the filling has set and lightly browned. Cool in the tin. Remove from the tin onto a serving platter and sift the icing sugar over the top. Eat warm or cold.

Cheesecake

FIG TART

The moment I tasted this fig tart I wanted the recipe. Stephane McGlynn, executive head chef at Caviston Restaurant in Monkstown, County Dublin, kindly supplied it. It reflects Stephane's half Irish, half French culinary background. As the walled kitchen gardens of great Irish houses prove, figs will grow in the Irish climate – provided that they are planted against a south-facing wall to catch whatever sun is going, the soil is not too rich, and the roots are contained.

SERVES 6–8

Ingredients:

shortcrust pastry (recipe page ?) rolled out to fit a 23 cm/9 inch tart tin and baked blind

For the frangipane:

225 g/8 oz/2 generous US cups ground almonds

225 g/8 oz/1 generous US cup icing sugar flavoured with a vanilla pod

60 g/2 oz unsifted plain white flour

225 g/8 oz/2 sticks unsalted butter, softened

2 medium eggs

2-3 tablesp brandy

1 tablesp Amaretto liqueur, or a good dash of almond essence

For the marinated figs:

100 g/3^1/$_3$ oz/^{1}/$_2$ US cup caster sugar, flavoured with vanilla

the grated zest of 1 orange

a wine glass-full of red wine

300g/12 oz/6-8 fresh figs, halved

Method:

Stir the vanilla-flavoured caster sugar into the red wine until it is dissolved. Add the orange zest. Place the halved figs in this liquid and marinate for at least two hours.

Make the frangipane by beating the softened butter and the icing sugar together until pale and fluffy. Add the flour, almonds, eggs, brandy, Amaretto (or almond essence). Mix well. Spread this mixture on the baked blind shortcrust pastry case.

Drain the marinade from the figs. Making sure there is not too much liquid clinging to the fig halves, place them, cut face down, on the frangipane. Bake at 180°C/350°F/Gas 4 for 50–60 minutes. Once the top is browned it will be necessary to lay a piece of greaseproof paper over the tart to prevent the top turning too dark (or burning) before it is cooked through. It is done when a skewer inserted in the centre comes out clean. Best eaten warm and freshly baked. However it may also be re-warmed gently in the oven.

Figs

GUR CAKE

To a young Dublin jackeen, 'going on the gur' meant mitching from, skiving off, or taking an unauthorised day off, school. A wise 'gurrier' would have acquired the price of a piece of Gur cake to sustain him. Gur cake is, of course, an invention of commercial bakeries to use up unsold cakes and bread – by its very nature the taste and texture changed from day to day. Leftovers are mixed up, with a little extra dried fruit and enough water to bind the lot into a moist gunge (indeed, the Cork version was often called 'donkey's gunge'), sandwiched between two layers of robust pastry, baked, and then cut into good-sized chunks. This concoction, always the cheapest item on sale in the bakery shop, was much beloved of Dublin gurriers, especially when hot and steaming from the oven. Gur cake is still on sale in the city of Dublin, especially in The Liberties. Elsewhere, much the same cake goes by the grand title of 'fruit slice'. If you are thrifty and into recycling you might like to try this domestic version. It's good made with tired Christmas cake or pudding, with boiled fruit cake, brack, sponge cake and bread. Obviously, the more bread in the mixture the more dried fruit you need to add.

MAKES 8–12

Ingredients:

280g/10 oz shortcrust, or puff, pastry

About 350g/12 oz leftover cake and/or bread

60 g/2 oz/½ US cup unsifted self-raising white flour

90 g/3 oz/scant ½ US cup brown sugar

1 large egg, beaten (or the equivalent amount of milk or water) to mix

1-2 teasp mixed spice

60-175g/2-6 oz/¼-1 US cup mixed dried fruit, or to taste

Method:

Place the leftover cake and/or bread in a food processor and whiz until you have fairly fine crumbs. Stir in all the rest of the dry ingredients using as much fruit as you feel you need to achieve a rich fruity mixture. Add the egg (or milk or water) using as much liquid as will make a stiff paste-like mixture. Grease a rectangular tin about 25-28 cm/10-11 inches by 18-20 cm/ 7-8 inches wide. Roll out the pastry thinly into two pieces the size of the tin. Line the bottom of the tin with one layer of pastry. Spread the filling on top. Cover with the second layer of pastry. Prick the top all over (lightly) with a fork, then brush with a little milk. Bake at 190°C/375°F/Gas 5 for 45–55 minutes, or until crisp and golden brown. Cool in the tin.

Traditionally, gur cake is cut into rectangular chunks about 9cm/3½ inches long and 5 cm/2 inches wide.

MINCE PIES WITH IRISH WHISKEY

Mince pies were originally made with minced beef or lamb, mixed with spices and (when available) some fruit for flavouring. Over time the fruits became more important and the meat content was reduced. Nowadays the only element of meat in mincemeat is beef suet. It is hard to find ready-prepared suet but, given a little warning, any good, reputable craft butcher will provide you with a piece of fresh suet which can be easily grated with a coarse grater or chopped in a food processor. Although flaky (or puff) pastry was traditional for mince pies, it is very rich and high in fat; short crust pastry is more often used today.

MAKES 12 pies; About 2 x 450 g/1 lb jars mincemeat

Ingredients:

about 450 g/1 lb short crust pastry

For the mincemeat:

700 g/1½ lb/4 US cups dried fruit (equal proportions of sultanas, raisins and currants)

110 g/4 oz/¾ US cup mixed citrus peel (optional)

225 g/8 oz/a generous US cup moist dark-brown sugar (muscovado)

110 g/4 oz/1 US cup beef suet, shredded

60 g/2 oz/²/₃ US cup ground nuts (hazel or almonds)

1 large cooking apple, peeled, cored and finely chopped

1 teasp nutmeg, grated

½ teasp allspice, ground

½ teasp cinnamon, ground

1 lemon, zest and juice

125 ml/4 fl oz/½ US cup Irish whiskey

Method:

Make the filling two weeks in advance to allow the flavours to develop. In a large mixing bowl stir all the ingredients together until well mixed. Cover and leave in a cool place for 24 hours. Mix well again before potting into clean preserving jars. Cover tightly and store in a cool, dark place.

Lightly grease the base of a shallow 12-space bun tin. Roll out the pastry and use a 9 cm/3½ inch pastry cutter (or whatever size fits your bun tin) to cut out 24 rounds. Place one in each of twelve tins then fill it with about a heaped teaspoon of the mincemeat. Dampen the edges of each pastry case before placing the remaining twelve pastries on top as lids. Press the edges together to seal firmly. Bake at 220°C/425°F/Gas 7 for about 20 minutes or until golden-brown. Remove the pies from the tin carefully and place them to cool on a wire rack. Dust with icing sugar.

Mince pies must be served warm. They are wonderful served with a little whipped cream.

kerry apple cake

Kerry men (and women and children) are well-known inside and outside Ireland for having jokes told against them. Actually, I've always regarded this as the best Kerry joke of all because, in reality, Kerry people are famous for being 'cute' – clever, on the ball, always keeping the best things secret. In a Kerry apple cake the apples are 'invisible', their presence revealed only when you taste it.

SERVES 4–8

Ingredients:

3 large cooking apples, peeled, cored and diced

225 g/8 oz/2 US cups unsifted white flour

90 g/3 oz/¾ stick butter

90 g/3 oz/(scant) ½ US cup caster sugar

I teasp baking powder

¼ teasp salt

I extra-large egg, beaten

¼ teasp nutmeg, grated (or ground cinnamon or ground cloves)

3 tablesp Demerara sugar

Method:

Grease a 20 cm/8-inch cake tin with butter, then line it with greaseproof paper.

Sift the flour into a bowl and rub in the butter until you have a mixture like fine breadcrumbs. Mix the salt, sugar, and baking powder together in a small bowl, then stir into the flour mixture. Add the chopped apples and the egg and mix to a soft dough. Turn the dough into the cake tin. Mix the Demerara sugar and spice and sprinkle over the top of the cake. Bake at once at 180°C/350°F/Gas 4 for about 45 minutes, or until a skewer inserted into the middle of the cake comes out clean. Traditionally this cake is eaten hot from the oven. It can be served warm (even cold) as long as it is freshly made – just warm it gently if it is to be eaten the following day.

PORTER CAKE

Porter was a type of stout, weaker in alcohol content, but with the same dark colour and rich flavour as present-day stouts. Alas, porter is no longer widely available as the mainstream brewers abandoned it years ago. However, in recent years, two micro-breweries revived it. So look out for Biddy Early's Porter and Porterhouse Porter. Although most people now make this cake with stout, it's still called porter cake. Like many Irish dishes there is no definitive recipe – every province, parish and house puts its own spin on it. This particular recipe is that of Paula Daly, a famous Irish cook, who, through the medium of radio, taught many an Irishwoman not to fear baking!

Ingredients:

175 g/6 oz/1 generous US cup unsifted wholemeal flour

175 g/6 oz/1½ US cups unsifted plain white flour

1 teasp (rounded) mixed spice

1 teasp (level) baking powder

225 g/8 oz/1 generous US cup soft dark brown sugar

225 g/8 oz/2 sticks butter

3 large eggs, beaten

250 ml/8 fl oz/1 US cup porter or stout

175 g/6 oz/1 generous US cup raisins

175 g/6 oz/1 US cup sultanas

90 g/3 oz/¾ US cup walnuts, chopped

grated zest of an orange

Method:

Put the wholemeal flour in a bowl and sift the white flour, mixed spice and baking powder on top. Mix well. In another bowl, cream the butter and sugar until very light and fluffy. Add the eggs, a little at a time, beating well during and after each addition. Should the mixture curdle add a little flour. Gradually fold in the flour and stout, a little at a time. When everything is incorporated fold in the fruit, nuts and orange zest.

Turn into a tin (20 cm/8 inches square, or 23 cm/9 inches round) lined with greaseproof (unwaxed) paper. Smooth the top evenly with the back of a tablespoon, then bake on a low shelf in a preheated oven at 150°C/300°F/Gas 2 for 3¼–3½ hours.

Porter Cake

CIDER CAKE

Apples are a native fruit and cider has been made in Ireland since earliest times. There is still a thriving cider industry and the sight of apple orchards in blossom is uplifting in springtime. Cakes made with apples are traditional at Hallowe'en and on St Brigid's Day in February.

Ingredients:

110 g/4 oz/1 stick butter

110 g/4 oz/generous ½ US cup caster sugar

1 teasp bicarbonate of soda

225 g/8 oz/2 US cups unsifted self-raising white flour

½ teasp freshly grated nutmeg

2 medium eggs, beaten

200 ml/7 fl oz/generous ¾ US cup medium sweet cider

2 juicy eating apples, peeled, cored and sliced into wedges (optional)

1-2 tablesp caster sugar for the topping

Method:

Grease a 23 cm/9 inch square, non-stick baking tin with butter. Cream the butter and sugar until light and fluffy. Sift the flour, nutmeg and bicarbonate of soda together. Beat a tablespoon of the flour mix into the butter and sugar mixture followed by all the eggs. Mix in half the remaining flour. Add the cider and beat in fully. Mix in the rest of the flour. Pour the mixture into the tin. If using the apples insert the slices into the mixture (wide side facing upwards) in an even pattern. Bake immediately at 180°C/350°F/Gas 4 for 35–45 minutes or until the top is golden, the cake begins to shrink from the sides of the tin, and the top feels springy to the touch. Allow to cool slightly in the tin before turning out carefully. Place right side up and sprinkle the top with caster sugar. This cake is also lovely eaten as a dessert while still warm served with whipped cream.

Variation:

Replace the apple with peeled, sliced wedges of dessert pear.

GINGERBREAD

Just when you've got to grips with Irish people speaking of a soda 'cake' when they mean bread, they start calling this popular cake ginger 'bread'. There are dozens of variations on this soft, moist, sticky cake; some use more or less ginger, or treacle, or sometimes a combination of treacle and golden syrup; some are tray-baked in a Swiss roll tin, others are a tallish loaf shape (in a loaf tin).

Ingredients:

225 g/8 oz/1 generous US cup soft brown sugar

225 g/8 oz treacle

225 g/8 oz/2 sticks butter

350 g/12 oz/3 US cups unsifted plain white flour

2 teasp ginger, ground

1 tablesp cinnamon, ground

2 medium eggs, beaten

300 ml/10 fl oz/1¼ US cups milk

2 level teasp bicarbonate of soda

Method:

Preheat oven to 150°C/300°F/Gas 2. Grease and line a 30 x 20 cm/12 x 8 inch baking tin with greaseproof paper. In a pot, gently heat the sugar, butter and treacle until melted. Pour into a mixing bowl and cool to room temperature. Sift the flour and spices over this mixture and stir in, together with the eggs. Place the bicarbonate of soda in a jug. Warm the milk gently and when it reaches blood temperature pour it over the soda, stirring continuously; add at once to the cake mixture and mix well. Pour immediately into the baking tin. Bake for about 1 hour. After 45 minutes cover the top of the cake with greaseproof paper or tinfoil. The cake is done when the sides begin to shrink back from the edges of the tin and a skewer inserted in the centre comes out clean. Cool in the tin. When it is quite cold lift out, peel back the paper and serve cut into squares. Traditionally this already rich cake is eaten buttered.

Variation:

Substitute half the treacle for an equal quantity of golden syrup. It has a sweeter taste and is lighter in colour.

seedy cake

A plain cake enlivened only by the taste of caraway seeds. It was once a popular teatime treat particularly in southern counties. Traditionally it is not iced or decorated, except perhaps with some caraway seeds sprinkled on top, or a dusting of icing sugar.

SERVES 6–8

Ingredients:

110 g/4 oz/1 stick butter, softened slightly

110 g/4 oz/generous ½ US cup caster sugar

2 very large eggs, beaten

225 g/8 oz/2 US cups unsifted plain white flour

1 level teasp baking powder

½-1 tablesp caraway seeds (or to taste)

a little milk

Method:

Preheat oven to 180°C/350°F/Gas 4. Prepare a cake tin (about 18 cm/7 inches in diameter and 16 cm/6½ inches deep) by greasing the tin and then lining it with well-buttered greaseproof, or non-stick paper. Cream the butter and sugar until it is very light, fluffy, and pale in colour. Sift the flour and baking powder into a bowl. Taking a small amount at a time, mix the eggs along with a little flour into the butter and sugar mixture. When all the eggs have been incorporated add the remaining flour, the caraway seeds and just enough milk to make a mixture of soft, dropping consistency. Turn into the tin and smooth the top. Bake for about 15 minutes and then reduce the oven temperature to 160°C/325°F/Gas 3 and continue baking for about another hour. The cake should be well-risen, dark golden-brown in colour and have begun to shrink away from the sides of the tin. Cool in the tin for 15 minutes; then lift out and cool fully on a wire rack. Only when cold should you remove the paper.

Variation:

Irish spice cake is made in exactly the same way. Replace the caraway seeds with 1½-2 teasp mixed spice, sifted into the flour to ensure even distribution.

Cherry Cake

In a perfect cherry cake the fruit is suspended evenly throughout the cake and the crumb is buttery and moist. On the competitive baking circuit this is the one that sorts out novice bakers from those who know the tricks of the trade.

Ingredients:

280 g/10 oz/ generous 1½ US cups of whole glacé cherries

110 g/4 oz/1 generous US cup ground almonds

225 g/8 oz/2 US cups unsifted plain white flour

½ level (5 ml) teasp baking powder

225 g/8 oz/2 sticks unsalted butter, slightly softened

225 g/8 oz/1 generous US cup caster sugar

4 medium eggs, beaten

juice and finely grated zest of ½ a lemon, or a little milk

an extra tablesp of caster sugar for the topping

Method:

Grease and line the base and sides of a deep 20 cm/8 inch diameter cake tin. Quarter most of the cherries and toss in a bowl with the ground almonds. Sift the flour and baking powder together. Beat the sugar and butter together until pale, light and fluffy. Beat in the eggs, a little at a time, alternating each addition of egg with some of the flour mixture. When all the eggs are incorporated, fold in the remaining flour. Finally, carefully, mix in the cherry and almond mixture, the lemon juice and zest. Place mixture in the tin; smooth the top and press the remaining whole cherries into the top. Sprinkle with a tablespoon of caster sugar. Bake in the middle of the oven at 180°C/350°F/Gas 4 for one hour. Then open the oven door and gently rest a sheet of foil on the top of the tin; close the door very gently. Bake for about 30 minutes more, or until the cake has shrunk slightly from the sides of the tin and is springy to the touch when lightly pressed with the fingers. Cool in the tin for 15 minutes. Turn out carefully and allow to cool fully on a wire rack. When cold, remove the paper and store in an airtight cake tin. For best results allow 1–2 days for the cake to mature and moisten.

real egg sponge cake

This classic sponge cake contains no fat and is best eaten really fresh. The filling is very much a matter of what you fancy; whipped cream is traditional, usually with a layer of a red fruit jam added. Sometimes jam alone is used and, occasionally, lemon curd. It is never iced but simply finished with a layer of sifted icing sugar.

Ingredients:

For the cake:

90 g/3 oz/¾ US cup plain white flour

½ teasp baking powder

3 large eggs, separated

90 g/3 oz/ scant ½ US cup caster sugar

For the filling:

125 ml/4 fl oz/½ US cup whipped cream

3 tablesp jam, gently warmed

For the topping:

1-2 tablesp icing sugar, or caster sugar

Method:

Because this must be baked at once, first prepare two 18 cm/7 inch cake tins by greasing with butter and lining the base of the tins with greaseproof paper (which should also be greased). Sift the flour and baking powder together into a bowl and then return it to a wide, wire sieve. Place the egg whites in a large, completely grease-free mixing bowl. Place the yolks in a separate bowl. Add the sugar to the yolks and whisk with an electric mixer until very thick, pale and fluffy. This will take at least five minutes. Wash and dry the whisk very well to ensure that it is clean and grease-free.

Whisk the whites until stiff but not too dry. Use a large metal spoon to fold the sifted flour and the egg whites (alternately) into the egg yolk and sugar mixture. Try to finish with the last of the egg whites. Spoon equal quantities of the mixture into the prepared tins and bake on the middle shelf of the oven at 180°C/350°F/Gas 4 for 20–25 minutes. They are done when they feel springy on top and the sides have begun to shrink from the sides of the tins.

Allow the cakes to cool in the tin for about 3 minutes. If you wish to top with caster sugar turn one cake out onto a sheet of greaseproof paper sprinkled evenly with caster sugar and then place both (right side up) on a wire rack to cool fully.

When cold, spread the bottom layer of the cake with slightly warmed jam. Let it cool fully and then spread with whipped cream. Place the other layer on top. If topping with icing sugar, sift as much sugar as desired over the top of the cake.

Cooks Tip:

Stale sponge cake may be used to make Tipsy Cake (see recipe p.73)

Sponge Cake

CARROT CAKE

One of the most popular of modern Irish cakes — probably because people persuade themselves that carrots make it a health food!

Ingredients:

110 g/4 oz/1 stick unsalted butter, softened

90 g/3 oz/scant ½ cup light brown sugar or caster sugar

110 g/4 oz/1 cup unsifted self-raising flour

1 level teasp baking powder

2 medium eggs

2 tablesp ginger syrup (from the jar) or honey

2 tablesp stem ginger in syrup, drained and finely chopped

110 g/4 oz carrot, finely grated

2 level tablesp almonds, ground

For the icing:

125 g/4½ oz soft cream cheese

1-2 tablesp honey

1-2 tablesp almonds, chopped (optional)

Method:

Whisk together thoroughly the butter, sugar, flour, baking powder, eggs and ginger syrup or honey. You may do this in a food processor.

Mix the stem ginger, carrot and almonds and add to the cake mixture. Grease the bottom and sides of a 900g/2 lb loaf tin and line with greaseproof paper. Fill with the cake mixture, smoothing the top, and hollowing it slightly in the centre. Bake at 180°C/350°F/Gas 4 for about 55 minutes or until a skewer inserted in the centre comes out clean and the cake is beginning to shrink away from the sides of the tin. Cool in the tin before turning out. Do not ice until the cake is completely cold. Make the icing by beating together the soft cheese and honey. Spread this on the cake and, if you wish, sprinkle the top with the chopped almonds.

IRISh whISkey-feɔ ChRISTmAS CAKe

A well-loved tradition. Even people who don't bake much all year will try their hand at, or persuade a relative or friend to supply, this rich festive cake. This version is topped with fruit and nuts, although many people still adhere to the ritual of topping with marzipan and royal icing. For best results choose high quality dried fruit, sulphur-free, if possible.

Ingredients:

450 g/1 lb/3 US cups currants

175 g/6 oz/1 US cup sultanas

175 g/6 oz/1 scant US cup raisins

60 g/2 oz/¹/₃ US cup glacé cherries, washed and chopped

60 g/2 oz/¹/₃ US cup mixed citrus peel, finely chopped

225 g/8 oz/2 US cups unsifted plain white flour

1 teasp ground cinnamon

1 teasp ground nutmeg

1 teasp ground dry ginger

60 g/2 oz/scant ½ US cup chopped almonds

225 g/8 oz/1 generous US cup dark brown sugar

1 tablesp treacle, warmed

225 g/8 oz/2 sticks unsalted butter

3 large eggs

grated zest of 1 unwaxed lemon

grated zest of 1 unwaxed orange

3 tablesp Irish whiskey, and more to feed the cake

For the topping:

90 g/3 oz/½ US cup whole glacé cherries (both red and green)

90 g/3 oz/¾ US cup whole nuts (brazil and walnuts)

For the glaze:

250 ml/8 fl oz/1 US cup Irish cider

110 g/4 oz/generous ½ US cup caster sugar

Method:

The night before baking take all the dried fruit and sprinkle it with the whisky; cover and leave to absorb the flavour.

Grease a 20 cm/8-inch round (or an 18 cm/7 inch square) loose-based, deep, cake tin and line with greaseproof paper. Sift the flour and spices together into a bowl. Cream the butter and sugar together until very light, pale and fluffy. Beat one tablespoon of flour into the creamed butter and sugar, then beat in the eggs, one tablespoon at a time. Do this very thoroughly and, if the mixture appears to be splitting or curdling, add a little flour before the next addition of egg. Fold in the flour (no beating this time). Now stir in all the remaining ingredients. You will have a stiff mixture by now – if it seems too stiff add a little cider. Now is the time to call in the family to make their secret wishes as they give the cake a final stir. Place the mixture in the cake tin, spreading it out and making a depression in the centre (gently) with the back of a spoon.

It is traditional to tie a band of brown paper around the tin (an effort to prevent scorching) but few people bother. However, you should have a double thickness sheet of greaseproof paper at the ready to place on the top of the cake if the top is becoming too browned. Bake at 130°C/275°F/Gas 1 on a shelf below the middle of the oven for 4¼–4¾ hours. Do not on any account open the door of the oven in the early stages. After about 3 hours it is safe to check it at odd intervals and cover the top if it seems necessary. But close the oven door gently! The cake is done when you cannot hear a trace of a sizzling sound and a skewer inserted in the centre comes out clean. Cool in the tin.

Turn out, remove the paper, and wrap in a double thickness of fresh paper and store in a tin to mature for 6–8 weeks. Feed, at intervals, with Irish whiskey by making several holes in the top with a thin skewer or darning needle and dribbling in teaspoons of whiskey. Allow it to soak in, then re-wrap. At the next feeding time, do the bottom; and then do the sides.

A day or so before Christmas finish the cake. Place the sugar and cider together in a pot, bring to the boil, stirring, then reduce the heat and simmer until the liquid is reduced to about five tablespoons. Brush about half of this on the cake top; place the cherries and nuts in rows (or whatever pattern pleases you) and then use the remaining glaze to brush the fruit and nuts.

OATFLAKE AND WHEAT BISCUITS

This is a fairly sweet biscuit. If you don't have a sweet tooth you may reduce the amount of sugar.

MAKES 10–12

Ingredients:

110 g/4 oz/1 US cup fine-ground wholemeal flour

110 g/4 oz /1¹⁄₃ US cups oatflakes

110 g/4 oz/1 stick butter

110 g/4 oz/generous ½ US cup caster sugar

1 medium egg, beaten

½ teasp salt

½ teasp baking powder

Method:

Cream the butter and sugar until very pale, light and fluffy. Sift the fine wholemeal flour, the salt and the baking powder together, then stir into the mixture. Add the egg and the oatflakes. Mix well with your hands. Turn out the mixture onto a well-floured work surface and divide into two equal pieces, then roll out each until they are about ½ cm/¼ inch thick. Cut out the biscuits using a 5 cm/2 inch scone cutter. As you cut each one, place it on a greased baking tray. Incorporate any trimmings into the second piece of dough – the dough will not be harmed by repeated rolling – and repeat the cutting process. Bake on the middle shelf of the oven at 200°C/400°F/Gas 6 for about 15 minutes. You are aiming for a golden-brown colour. Beware, though, these biscuits will burn quickly, so watch them carefully towards the end of the cooking time.

CRUNCH MUNCH BISCUITS

When children first get the baking bug (and they all do, given the slightest encouragement) generations of Irish mothers have set them to make these simple biscuits. The hard part (for the child) is waiting until they're cooled and crisp before eating them. In the unlikely event that there are any left over, they should be stored in an airtight tin or they will go soft again.

MAKES 12–16

Ingredients:

150 g/5 oz/1¼ sticks butter

2½ tablesp golden syrup

90 g/3 oz/scant ½ US cup caster sugar

150 g/5 oz/1¼ US cups unsifted plain white flour

½ teasp bicarbonate of soda

110 g/4 oz/1⅓ US cups oatflakes

3-4 tablesp milk

Method:

Sift flour and bicarbonate of soda together and set aside. In a large pot over a gentle heat melt the butter, golden syrup and sugar slowly until you have a syrupy liquid. Add all the other ingredients but use only enough milk to bind the ingredients into a stiff paste when pressed firmly with the hands. Cool in the fridge until the mixture is just warm to the touch. Grease a couple of baking trays. Take pieces the size of a walnut, flatten them slightly with your fingers and place them, spaced well apart, on the trays. They spread as they cook so you must leave room between them. Bake near the centre of the oven at 160°C/325°F/Gas 3 for about 30 minutes, turning the trays round at least once so that the biscuits brown evenly. They will be soft and break easily at this stage so lift them from the tray with a palette knife (or a fish slice) and place on a wire rack to cool and become crisp.

ḣALLOWE'EN PUᎠᎠᏆNG

This pudding is eaten at Hallowe'en in the Lower Ards area of Ulster. It could also make a lighter alternative to traditional Christmas pudding. 'Favours', which always including a ring – often a brass curtain ring – are placed in the pudding at Hallowe'en (for safety wrap this in greaseproof paper). The recipe was given to me by well-known food writer Honor Moore who hails from Newtownards and is a fund of knowledge on Ulster baking traditions.

SERVES 4–6

Ingredients:

60 g/2 oz/½ US cup unsifted white flour

90 g/3 oz/¾ stick butter, cut into small dice

110 g/4 oz/1 US cup wholemeal breadcrumbs

½ teasp bicarbonate of soda

1 teasp mixed spice

½ teasp salt

60 g/2 oz/¼ US cup caster sugar

225 g/8 oz/1¼ US cups mixed dried fruit

1 tablesp treacle

175 ml/6 fl oz/¾ US cup buttermilk

Method:

Sift the flour and place in a mixing bowl with the butter. Rub the butter into the flour until the mixture resembles breadcrumbs. Sift the soda, mixed spice and salt together and mix thoroughly into the flour mixture. Add all the other ingredients, using just enough buttermilk to give a soft but not sloppy mixture. Grease a 1 litre/2 lb/2 pint pudding bowl with butter (it should be large enough to allow the mixture to expand). Cover with a double thickness of greaseproof paper, making a pleat in the middle. Tie tightly with string, looping it across the centre to make a handle with which to lift the cooked pudding from the pot. Steam for about 3 hours.

Serve hot with whipped, fresh cream.

chRISTMAS PUDDING

Christmas pudding was first served, as far as written accounts record, to William the Conqueror by his chef Robert Argyllion on the occasion of his coronation in 1066. No doubt it came to Ireland by way of our own Norman conquerors. It's a dish that has taken many twists and turns down the years: once it was a kind of meat stew; by Elizabethan times it had become a meat porridge sweetened with fruit; a century later it had solidified into the dark, rich pudding we know today.

MAKES 5 x 450 g/1lb puddings or about 20 individual puddings

Ingredients:

225 g/8 oz/2 US cups beef suet, weighed when shredded

225 g/8 oz/2 US cups self-raising flour, unsifted

225 g/8 oz/4 US cups fresh white breadcrumbs

225 g/8 oz/1¼ US cups stoned prunes, chopped finely

225 g/8 oz/1½ US cups currants

225 g/8 oz/1¼ US cups raisins

225 g/8 oz/1¼ US cups sultanas

225 g/8 oz/1 generous US cup soft, dark brown sugar

110 g/4 oz/½ US cup glacé (candied) cherries, washed and chopped

110 g/4 oz/½ US cup mixed (candied) peel, chopped

1 cooking apple, peeled and grated

1 carrot, peeled and grated

1 unwaxed lemon, grated zest and juice

1 unwaxed orange, grated zest and juice

6 medium-sized eggs, beaten

1 teasp mixed spice/allspice

½ teasp nutmeg, grated

½ teasp cinnamon, ground

1 teasp salt

300 ml/10 fl oz/1¼ US cups stout

Method:

Sift flour and spices together into a large mixing bowl. Mix in suet, breadcrumbs, dried fruits and sugar. Stir in the salt, peel, cherries, carrot and apple. Mix in eggs, stout, orange, lemon zest and juice. Fill mixture into bowls, leaving 5cm (2 inches) headspace for rising. Cover with two layers of greaseproof paper, leaving a pleat in the centre. Tie tightly, arranging a handle on the top for lifting from the pot. Top with foil. Place in a steamer or pot with the water coming halfway up the bowl. Steam, covered, for 6–7 hours, topping up with boiling water as needed.

For the individual, small puddings, place in a roasting tin (with water coming halfway up the containers), cover with a tent of tin foil, shiny side down, and steam in an oven set at 150°C/300°F/Gas 2 for 1½ hours.

To reheat: Cover with fresh paper and string. Steam a large pudding for 2–3 hours, individual ones for 1 hour.

Serve with plain, unsweetened whipped cream, or clotted cream.

Cook's Tip:

Unless you have a big family or a large number of guests for Christmas, there will be leftover pudding to deal with. In Dublin, wedges of pudding are fried gently in butter until hot through.

A more interesting approach is to take about 225 g/8 oz cold pudding, crumbed as fine as possible, and mix into a litre of slightly softened ice cream. Refreeze at once.

Christmas Pudding

BRACK AND BUTTER PUDDING

Quicker to make and tastier than plain bread and butter pudding, this is also a thrifty way of using up stale barm brack.

SERVES 4–6

Ingredients:

225 g/8 oz brack (see recipe p. 30)

60 g/2 oz/½ stick butter

4 eggs

3 egg yolks

750 ml/1 ¼ pints/3 US cups milk

60 g/2 oz/(scant) ¼ US cup sugar

2 teasp vanilla essence

Method:

Cut the brack into slices about 1 cm/½ inch thick; cut these in half and butter. Take a large shallow dish (about 1.75 litres/3 pint capacity), grease it with butter, then arrange the slices of brack in it, buttered side up, overlapping just a little. Mix together the eggs, egg yolks, sugar, vanilla essence and milk, and strain this over the slices of brack. Allow to stand in a cool place for half an hour. Place the dish in a water bath (a roasting tin about half-filled with hot water) and bake at 170°C/325°F/Gas 3 for about an hour (or until the custard is set). Serve hot.

SPICED BREAD AND BUTTER PUDDING WITH IRISH WHISKEY CUSTARD

This recipe comes courtesy of renowned Irish chef Derry Clarke of L'Écrivain Restaurant in Dublin. It was created for an Irish Food Writers Guild Food Awards luncheon.

SERVES 6

Ingredients:
For the pudding:

8 slices of two-day-old white bread, crusts removed

225 g/8 oz/2 sticks unsalted butter

¼ teasp cinnamon, ground

¼ teasp mixed spice, ground

¼ teasp nutmeg, freshly grated

4 tablesp raisins

½ tablesp brown sugar

For the custard:

6 egg yolks

110 g/4 oz/generous ½ US cup caster sugar

½ a vanilla pod, or 1 teasp vanilla essence

500 ml/16 fl oz/2 US cups cream

30-60 ml/1-2 fl oz/⅛-¼ US cup Irish whiskey, to taste

Method:

Make the custard by beating the egg yolks and sugar together. In a saucepan bring the cream and vanilla to boiling point but do not allow to boil. Pour the cream over the eggs and beat at once until well mixed. Set aside. Melt the butter and spices together and set aside. Take a very large piece of cling film and use it to line the base and sides of a 900 ml/2 pint terrine, or loaf tin. Cut the bread so that it will fit the tin snugly. Lay a layer of bread on the base and brush it generously with the spiced butter mixture. Sprinkle with some of the raisins. Next spoon over a thin layer of the custard. Repeat these layers until the dish is full. Dust the top with the brown sugar. Set aside the remaining custard as this will be used for the sauce. Place the tin in a water bath (*bain marie*) and bake in a very low oven set to 110°C/225°F/Gas ¼ for one hour. Remove from the oven and allow to cool slightly. Carefully remove the pudding from the tin and peel off the cling film. Cut into slices for serving. Whisk the whiskey (to taste) into the remaining custard and cook slowly over a very gentle heat until the mixture coats the back of a spoon. Serve the slices of pudding with a little custard. If you wish, serve a scoop of apricot or vanilla ice cream with it.

sparkling trifle

Another recipe created for an Irish Food Writers Guild Food Awards luncheon by leading Irish chef Ross Lewis of Chapter One Restaurant (located under the Irish Writers' Museum in Dublin).

SERVES 6

Ingredients:

300 ml/10 fl oz/1¼ US cups double cream

1 vanilla pod

60 ml/2 fl oz/¼ US cup Amaretto liqueur

60 g/2 oz/generous ¼ US cup caster sugar

4 egg yolks

375 ml/12 fl oz/1½ US cups sparkling wine

1½ teasp gelatine, powdered

225 g/8 oz lemon sponge cake

255 g/9 oz mascarpone cheese

grated zest of one lemon

2 teasp flaked almonds, chopped

60 g/2 oz dark chocolate, chilled

Method:

Split the vanilla pod in half and discard the seeds. Place the pod in a saucepan with the cream and Amaretto liqueur and bring slowly just to boiling point. Remove from the heat and set aside to infuse. When fully cold remove the vanilla pod.

Beat the egg yolks and sugar together until pale and slightly thickened. Beat in the infused cream, a little at a time, until evenly combined. Rinse out the saucepan and return the mixture to it. Place over a very low heat and cook gently for about 10 minutes, stirring all the time with a wooden spoon. Cook only until the custard thickens slightly, just enough to coat the back of the spoon. Strain at once through a sieve into a cold bowl (to prevent further cooking). Whisk occasionally as it cools to prevent a skin forming. When cold, cover with cling film and chill overnight.

Make the wine jelly by soaking the powdered gelatine in two tablespoons of water. After 10 minutes it will have softened. Place the sparkling wine in a bowl in a saucepan and bring to simmering point. Add the soaked gelatine and stir until dissolved. Then remove from the heat at once.

Slice the lemon sponge cake thinly and arrange in overlapping layers in a wide wine glass. Spoon over the still unset jelly and chill for one hour to set.

Blanch the lemon zest briefly, refresh under cool water and dry. Beat the mascarpone to loosen it and add the lemon zest. Spread this over the jelly in an even layer. Chill for one hour. Whisk the cooled custard briefly and pour this over the mascarpone. Cover with cling film and chill overnight. Toast the almonds lightly and cool. Just before serving, cut slivers of the chocolate and use these and the almonds to decorate the top of the trifle.

Note: if the wine jelly is too extravagant use the same quantity of lemon jelly instead.

trifle

TIPSY CAKE

Not really a cake but a type of alcoholic fruit flan, this is the kind of dessert that can start out as an economy measure to use up stale sponge cake and whatever fruit is to hand. Peaches, nectarines, apricots, pears, mandarin oranges, tangerines would be typical of the type of fruit used.

SERVES 4–6

Ingredients:

175 g/6 oz stale real egg sponge cake, or trifle sponges

125 ml/4 fl oz/½ US cup medium dry sherry

450 g/1 lb/about 3 cups fresh fruit of your choice

250 ml/8 fl oz/1 US cup double cream, whipped

2 tablesp flaked almonds, lightly toasted

Method:

In a large, flat dish place one layer of sponge cake (filling side up if you are using leftover filled sponge cake). Drizzle the sherry evenly over the sponge cake. Prepare the fruit and dice into smallish cubes, taking care to retain all the juices. Spread fruit and juice in a thick layer over the soaked sponge. Next spread the whipped cream evenly over the top and finish by sprinkling the toasted almonds on top. Chill for at least an hour to allow the flavours to mingle.

ḣazlenut ṁeringue roulaḋe wiṫḣ raspḃerry sauce

This recipe comes from Sinead Bryne who, together with her husband, runs Lennon's Café-bar in Carlow Town. Recently she won the top prize in The Pub Lunch Awards. This gorgeous meringue uses hazelnuts from a native tree that has grown in Ireland for thousands of years. The nuts were a favoured food of the first hunter-gathers who arrived here after the last Ice Age. Raspberries, a native fruit that thrives in the Irish climate, make a light and delicious sauce for this lovely pudding/dessert.

Ingreḋients:

For ṫḣe roulaḋe:

6 (medium) egg whites

350 g/12 oz/about 1¾ US cups caster sugar

150 g/5 oz/1 US cup whole, shelled hazelnuts

300 ml/10 fl oz/1¼ US cups double cream, whipped

For ṫḣe sauce:

225 g/8 oz fresh raspberries

icing sugar to taste

METHOD:

First prepare the baking tin. Take a 30 cm x 23 cm/12 inch x 9 inch Swiss roll tin and line it with non-stick baking paper. Whisk the egg whites until they stand in stiff peaks. Gradually whisk in half the sugar and then fold in the remainder using a metal spoon. Turn into the prepared tin and spread evenly. Bake at 150°C/300°F/Gas 2 for one hour.

Meanwhile place the hazelnuts on a tray and roast in the oven until darkish brown. Cool slightly and remove the papery husks by rolling vigorously in a clean tea towel. Chop roughly. (If you wish, you can buzz briefly in a food processor. However, do take care to stop as soon as the nuts are coarsely chopped. If they are too finely chopped they will release their natural oil and neither the taste nor texture will be correct.)

Take a fresh sheet of non-stick baking paper and when the meringue is cooked turn it out carefully on to this sheet. Peel off the paper used to line the baking tin. Spread the whipped cream over the meringue and then sprinkle the chopped hazelnuts evenly over the top. Roll up carefully.

This is good served with a raspberry sauce – simply purée raspberries through a food mill and sweeten to taste with a little icing sugar.

Meringues

BLACKBERRY AND APPLE CRUMBLE

Fruit crumbles are rightly popular, being quicker to prepare than tarts or pies. Apples lead the list, followed closely (when in season) by a combination of blackberries and apple (illustrated on front cover), rhubarb, plums, and gooseberries. Use cooking apples rather than dessert apples. A variety called Bramley is best as it cooks to a fluffy texture and has a great taste. The addition of oatflakes is both traditional and gives an especially crunchy crumble topping.

Ingredients:

700 g/1½ lb cooking apples (or fruit of your choice)

225 g/8 oz blackberries

110 g/4 oz/generous ½ US cup sugar (or to taste)

a few cloves, or ½ teasp freshly ground nutmeg

For the crumble:

110 g/4 oz/1 US cup unsifted plain white flour

60 g/2 oz/²/₃ US cup oatflakes

90 g/3 oz/¾ stick butter, chopped

90 g/3 oz/scant ½ US cup light brown sugar

Method:

Peel, core and slice the apples into wedges. Place in an oval or rectangular pie dish with the blackberries. Sprinkle the sugar and spice on top. If you have a sweet tooth use the full amount. Rub the butter into the flour. Add the sugar and oatflakes and mix well, pressing it lightly together. Spread this evenly over the fruit. Bake at 180°C/350°F/Gas 4 for 40–45 minutes or until the crumble is golden brown and the fruit tender. Serve hot with whipped cream.

Alternative crumble topping:

175 g/6 oz/1½ US cups unsifted plain flour

90 g/3 oz/¾ stick butter

90 g/3 oz/scant ½ cup Demerara sugar

60 g/2 oz/½ cup walnuts, chopped

Rub the butter into the flour and then mix in the sugar and chopped walnuts. Spread on top of filling and press down lightly.

Glossary

The names used in Ireland for various types of flour are different from those used in the United States.

Wholemeal flour is just that – flour containing all the bran and germ. It comes in different grades: coarse, medium, or fine ground and which you use is a matter of taste. Some people prefer to use wheatmeal, a flour that has had some of the bran and germ removed, making it finer but less nutritious. Strong flour with a high gluten content is used for yeast breads; it is roughly the same as US bread flour with 12-14% protein. The recipes in this book refer to unbleached strong flour with no improvers or other additives.

Plain white flour is made with a blend of hard and soft wheat and has a protein content of 10-12%. In strength it lies between American all-purpose flour and American cake flour. In Ireland it is used for soda breads, tea breads, scones, pastry and cakes.

Self raising flour (called self rising in the US) is simply plain white flour with baking powder (and sometimes other chemical raising agents) added. It is sometimes used for scones and dropped scones.

Names aside, flours from different countries are liable to absorb liquid at different rates; even in Ireland different brands of flour will behave in this way. The relative levels of humidity in the atmosphere also have an effect on how much liquid is absorbed by flour – it's a fact of baking life. For this reason almost all the recipes in the book suggest approximate rather than precise amounts of liquid. Better results are likely to be got if you follow the directions for the type of dough or batter you are aiming for – a firm or a soft dough, or a thin or a thick batter. Because it is easier to add liquid than to incorporate extra flour, most of the recipes suggest adding 'enough liquid to make a firm/soft dough'. After you've made a recipe a few times you will get know how much liquid the flour you are using will absorb. A final word: usually, if a dough is made in a food processor, it needs rather less liquid.

Note on Oat Bread

Three products made from oats are used in Irish baking. Pinhead oatmeal, where the oat kernel is cut in half and the floury meal sifted out, is used to add flavour and texture to breads. When oats are ground they are called oatmeal or oatmeal flour. Coarse or rough oatmeal may be used for oatcakes. Medium and fine oatmeal are used widely in baking. Oatflakes (developed in America where they are called rolled oats) are made by steaming and rolling pinhead oatmeal. They are used in Irish baking for crumble toppings, in biscuits and, occasionally, to add texture to wholemeal breads. Oats have almost no gluten and used on their own make a very heavy bread, but one that is highly nutritious, with 16% protein.

Names of flours

Irish English / American English

Plain white flour / all-purpose or soft flour

Self raising flour / self rising flour

Strong flour / bread or hard wheat flour

Wholemeal flour / whole wheat flour

Oatmeal / oat flour

Oatflakes or flakemeal / rolled oats

Cornflour / cornstarch

Polenta or maize flour / cornmeal

Other Ingredients

Irish English / American English

Bicarbonate of soda / baking soda

Baking powder / double action baking powder

Baking tray / cookie or cake sheet

Biscuit / cookie

Butter, unsalted / sweet butter

Cider / hard cider

Cake mixture / cake batter

Cake tin / cake pan

Cherries, glacé / candied cherries

Cheese, mature or vintage cheddar / sharp or mature cheese

Cling film or clingwrap / plastic wrap

Crystallised fruit / candied fruit

Cream / single or light cream

Cream double / heavy whipping cream

Curd or cream cheese / soft cheese

Essence / extract

Hazelnut / filbert or cob nuts

Icing / frosting

Kitchen paper / paper towels

Lard / processed pig fat

Loaf tin / bread pan

Milk, full fat / whole milk

Mixed peel / citrons

Mixed spice / allspice

Muffins / English muffins

Muslin or butter muslin / cheesecloth

Pancake / crepe

Pastry case / pie shell or crust

Pastry cutter / biscuit or cookie cutter

Raisins / black raisins

Scone / biscuit

Shortcrust pastry / pie dough

Swiss roll tin / jelly roll pan

Tart or flan tin / quiche pan

Treacle / molasses

Vanilla pod / vanilla bean

Sugars:

Brown sugar, light / light golden soft sugar

Caster sugar / superfine sugar

Demerara sugar / turbibado sugar

Icing sugar / confectioners sugar

Soft brown sugar / dark rich soft sugar

Yeasts:

Dried yeast /yeast, active dry

Easy bake or quick action yeast / quick rise or rapid rise yeast

Weights and Measures

This is a table of the scale of equivalents used in this book. It is quite simply impossible to provide exact equivalents. Always use one system, either imperial or metric – never use a combination.

Metric / Imperial

7 g / ¼ oz	150 g / 5 oz	310 g / 11 oz	700 g / 1½ lb
15 g / ½ oz	175 g / 6 oz	350 g / 12 oz	900 g / 2 lb
30 g / 1 oz	200 g / 7 oz	380 g / 13 oz	1.1 kg / 2½ lb
60 g / 2 oz	225 g / 8 oz	400 g / 14 oz	1.4 kg / 3 lb
90 g / 3 oz	255 g / 9 oz	425 g / 15 oz	2 Kg / 4½ lb
110 g / 4 oz	280 g / 10 oz	450 g / 16 oz (1 lb)	

Liquids: Metric /Imperial / US cup measurements

15 ml / ½ fl oz / 1 (15ml) tablesp

30 ml / 1 fl oz / 2 tablesp or ⅛ cup

60 ml / 2 fl oz / ¼ cup

90 ml / 3 fl oz / ⅜ cup

125 ml / 4 fl oz / ½ cup

150 ml / 5 fl oz / ⅔ cup

175 ml / 6 fl oz / ¾ cup

250 ml / 8 fl oz / 1 cup (½ US pint)

300 ml / 10 fl oz (½ Imperial pint) / 1¼ US cup

375 ml / 12 fl oz / 1½ US cups

500 ml / 16 fl oz / 2 US cups (1 US pint)

1 litre / 1¾ Imperial pints / 4 cups (1 US quart)

Spoon measurements

Note that a teaspoon is 5 ml and a tablespoon 15 ml. In Irish baking recipes spoon measurements are taken to be gently rounded unless stated otherwise.

Cup measurements

There is wide variation between the volumes of different ingredients; for example, a cup of flour weighs just 110 g while sugar weighs 200 g. This has been taken into account when giving the equivalent American cup measurements. In Ireland ingredients, particularly for baking (which requires accuracy) are always measured by weight (originally using Imperial but now metric). As a member of the European Union where food ingredients are sold in metric quantities, most Irish recipes now take account of this fact.

Oven equivalent temperatures used:

°C / °F / Gas mark	
110 / 225 / Gas ¼	190 / 375 / Gas 5
140 / 275 / Gas 1	200 / 400 / Gas 6
150 / 300 / Gas 2	220 / 425 / Gas 7
160 / 325 / Gas 3	230 / 450 / Gas 8
180 / 350 / Gas 4	250 / 475 / Gas 9

All temperatures given are for conventional ovens. Fan-assisted ovens usually require a lower temperature and, often, a shorter cooking time. As these cookers vary, it is necessary to consult the instruction manual of the cooker used.